WOMEN CONSCIENTI
AN ANTHC

Edited by Ellen Elster and

Preface by Cynthia Enloe

PUBLISHED BY WAR RESISTERS' INTERNATIONAL

April 2010

ISBN 978-0-903517-22-5

CREDITS

Editorial Committee
Ellen Elster
Majken Jul Sørensen

Coordination
Ellen Elster
Majken Jul Sørensen
Andreas Speck

Editorial consultant
Mitzi Bales

Proofreading
Albert Beale

Layout
Andreas Speck

Cover design
Hilal Demir

Special thanks go to Marie Marcks for permission to reprint her drawing on page 22. Copyright — © Marie Marcks, Heidelberg, Germany (not covered by Creative Commons Licence — reprint only with the explicit permission of the copyright holder).

Thanks go to the *Irene Bruegel Feminist Fund* for financial support to printing this anthology.

CONTENTS

Publisher's Preface

Howard Clark, chair of War Resisters' International

When apartheid South Africa made it illegal to advocate conscientious objection, it was a woman — *Sheena Duncan*, president of the *Black Sash* — who saw the opportunity: that it remained legal to campaign against conscription and that such a campaign would have the potential to open a new front in the struggle for a non-racist South Africa. Opposing conscription could bring together a broad platform of social groups, especially in the white community (as only whites were conscripted), while demonstrating that a section of that community saw the struggle against apartheid as a common struggle. In 1983 *Black Sash*'s annual assembly called for a campaign against conscription, thereby triggering the foundation in 1984 of the *End Conscription Campaign* (ECC). Banned in 1986, it nevertheless continued — in cooperation with the existing network of *Conscientious Objector Support Groups* — to orchestrate white resistance to apartheid militarism until the system collapsed. Although only men were called up and therefore only men imprisoned as conscientious objectors, tens of women in the ECC were detained — some for months — in the 1980s.

This was by no means the first time women had taken the lead in campaigning against military recruitment. There were two little-known massacres in 18th century Britain — in Hexham, England, in 1761 and Tranent in Scotland in 1797 — where troops were sent in to crush anti-recruitment protests in which women were prime movers and in which a number of them were killed. During the first world war, women founded two of the main anti-recruitment campaigns in the USA — in 1915 *Jessie Wallace Hughan* (later founder of the *War Resisters League*) launched the *Anti-Enlistment League* and in 1917 *Emma Goldman* founded the *No Conscription League*. Meanwhile in Australia, the *Women's Peace Army* spearheaded the campaign that successfully defeated the government in two referendums, in 1916 and 1917, that would have brought in conscription for overseas service.

In several senses, an anthology such as this is long overdue. First in the sense of acknowledging this part of the relatively hidden history of antimilitarism. Second for War Resisters' International organisationally. Founded in 1921, WRI has for much of its history been male-dominated, despite the prominent role of women in various affiliates and with certain exceptions at the international level such as long-serving WRI General Secretary *Grace Beaton*. Since 1972 conscious efforts have been made to change this — first the introduction of inclusive language (s/he, etc), and then, beginning in 1976, the organisation of special women's gatherings, usually in conjunction with WRI's "elder sister" the *International Fellowship of Reconciliation*. The second gathering in Scotland served as a prelude to the resurgence of an international women's peace movement in the 1980s, and produced a forceful statement on Women as Total Resisters. The British women involved in these gatherings formed the *Feminism and Nonviolence Study Group* and WRI later co-published their book *Piecing It Together* (now online at http://wri-irg.org/pubs/Feminism_and_Nonviolence). Then in 1986 the WRI Women's Working Group was formed to take this work forward and to provide a welcoming entry point for women activists, while WRI's 1987 seminar on *Refusing War Preparations: Non-cooperation and Conscientious Objection* was a response to feminist prompting to look at *"the wider implications of conscientious objection"*. That seminar reflected new interest in the Anti-War Plan presented to WRI in 1934 by *Bart de Ligt*, but it took a decidedly more feminist approach. Activities central to war refusal — war tax resistance, refusing war work and opposing cultural preparations for war — are all areas where women have been and remain at the forefront.

A third and more immediate sense of this anthology being overdue is that its gestation has been rather protracted. Conceived as part of WRI's *Right to Refuse to Kill* (RRTK) programme, there was at one point an intention of presenting the anthology at the 2007 seminar on Gender and Militarism, organised by WRI and its Israeli affiliate *New Profile*. It appears now largely thanks to the persistence of two patient mid-wives, *Ellen Elster* and *Majken Jul Sørensen* — both members of the WRI Executive committee that decided to publish the anthology — and to the typically conscientious support of the RRTK programme worker in the WRI office, *Andreas Speck*. The publication of this anthology is a sign of WRI's continued commitment to bring together and support women objectors and to address issues of gender and militarism, both in the WRI's staffed programmes — the RRTK programme itself, and *Nonviolence for a Change*, promoting nonviolent action to remove the causes of war — and more generally throughout the WRI network.

Preface

By Cynthia Enloe

Central bankers. The very idea of central bankers has become so deeply masculinized that most of us don't add a gendered adjective. We don't say *"male central bankers"*. We only add a gendered descriptor on that rare occasion when a woman has been appointed to head the country's central bank. Then we feel compelled to say *"female central banker"*. The same holds true today with other categories of actors — 747 pilots, football stars, hedge fund brokers, police chiefs, bulldozer operators, gangsters, firefighters, finance ministers. The good news — a sign of progress — is that nowadays there are women here and there who have broken into these masculinized ranks. *"Woman pilot"* no longer sounds like a total oxymoron. Thanks to organized political pressure and their own sheer grit, there are today handfuls of women in each one of these masculinized roles, but they remain so unusual that we usually feel we need to say *"woman finance minister"* or *"woman firefighter"*. Otherwise, when talking just about an *"ordinary"* finance minister or firefighter, we drop the gender reference. No need. Everyone knows that they usually are men.

Much the same is true for how most of us think about conscientious objectors. An *"ordinary"* conscientious objector is presumably male. You presume it. I presume it. So, no need for either of us to say *"male conscientious objector"*, to distinguish a particular male resister from a female resister. It is our own habit of masculinizing not only soldiers, but also those who resist soldiering, that has made this new book so important for its contributors to create and for us to read.

Yet there is more to this book than just making visible — de-exoticizing — women conscientious objectors. In addition, this book, read cover-to-cover (not just cherry-picked), reveals how loosening the ropes that tie masculinity to soldiering, and masculinity to resistance to soldiering, makes us smarter about both the subtle workings of masculinity and of militarization — and to the reliance of each on the other. Any analysis that exposes reliance of one thing on another serves to make each more vulnerable, each more open to challenge and to potential transformation. The contributors to this collection shine bright lights on the root system of militarization that stubbornly sustains militaries, soldiering, and the preparation for and the waging of wars.

It has been feminist-informed women — ie women who openly investigate patriarchy's daily operations — within national and international conscientious objector movements who have helped persuade so many men considering conscientious objection to seriously confront their own stakes in particular forms of patriarchal masculinity. They have shown us that conscientious objector movements, whose participants imagine that focusing on class inequalities, colonialism, capitalism and racism — each indeed crucial to candidly explore — is

11

sufficient, turn out to be conscientious objector movements which stop at the water's edge. They are anti-war movements whose leaders and supporters hesitate to wade into the strong tides of patriarchy. In fact, in their reluctance they may actually reinforce it, reinvigorating patriarchy's privileging of masculinity. The result of these personal and collective political and personal hesitations too often is that one of the key dynamics sustaining not only the privileging of soldiering, but also the deeper structures of militarism, is left securely in place, ready for service in the next war.

Only recently, I confess, have I become aware of the mind-changing, movement-altering work of women as conscientious objectors. While I have been taught by several generations of feminist colleagues to pay close attention to the histories of women as peace activists, I still too often thought of those women active in specifically conscientious objector movements — in World War I Britain, in apartheid-era South Africa, during the Vietnam War years in the US — chiefly as supporters. These were the women, I imagined, who gave backing to brothers and boy friends who had chosen to resist the government's compulsory male military conscription; these were the women who had become activists within male-led, male-conceptualized anti-conscription movements. My imaginings of these women were limited by my own insufficient feminist curiosity. I didn't ask enough about how a seemingly righteous cause might be infected with its own brand of patriarchy, how its seemingly courageous participants might be reliant on women remaining comfortably (for them) feminine, nurturing and supporting the masculinized cause, but not shaping its strategies, much less its understandings. In fact, feminists active inside conscientious objector movements had more than nurturing support to offer; they had fundamental insights.

Three recent experiences opened my eyes, enlivened my feminist curiosity. They all came quite close together. The first came as I read the work-in-progress of a friend, the South Korean feminist scholar/activist, *Insook Kwon*. Insook, who already had explored the surprisingly militarized internal dynamics of South Korea's 1980s pro-democracy movement which succeeded in ending decades of military rule, now turned her keen intelligence to the country's continuing male conscription system. She asked questions flowing from her feminist curiosity. She made explicit the workings of both femininity and masculinity inside the legal system and the country's wider political culture that supported South Korea's conscription processes. She reminded me that male military conscription was a feminist issue.

The second experience came soon after, during a trip to Israel in which I was asked to speak to — and, more importantly, listen to, learn from — Israeli Women's Studies scholars and feminist activists who were charting and questioning their society's profound militarization. *New Profile* was one of the groups whose work I'd followed for several years. Started by a group of Israeli middle-aged women, some of whom had themselves done military service, most of whom had had sons and daughters eligible for military conscription, *New Profile*'s members had come together to share with each other their concerns about — and to figure out how to take responsibility for — militarization's myriad strands in their lives.

By the time I visited *New Profile*'s activists, they had launched a youth group, bringing young women and men into their discussions and their actions. Military service — its rationales, its consequences for both young people and their mothers and fathers, and its connecting links to other cultural and economic dynamics in society — always was on the agenda.

During my short visit *Idan Halili* was making a public stand against her military call-up. Her friend and supporter *Tali Lerner* brought Idan's ideas into the *New Profile* conversations. Idan cited *Virginia Woolf* as she explained how, step by step, as a young girl and then as a teenager she had come to her own decision to reject the government's military call-up when it came. Later, at a lively inter-generational gathering in Tel Aviv, Idan went on to explain why she did not want to be seen as a "hero". She did not want her enduring a prison sentence to be thought of by any peace activists as particularly courageous. Doing either, she warned us all, would be encouraging a sort of privileging that, even when attached to a young woman, would feed masculinized hierarchies.

During this same period, I was invited to spend time in Turkey. Thanks to the welcoming guidance of scholar/activist *Ayşe Gül Altınay*, I met scores of Turkish feminist intellectuals and activists, among them *Ferda Ülker*. Ferda was part of a group of women in the coastal city of Izmir who recently had decided that women active in a local mixed-gender group supporting those men resisting military conscription had reached the point in their own on-going journeys toward awareness where they needed to have their own space. They wanted to dig deeper into the connections they were beginning to see between masculinities, femininities, conscription, militarization and anti-militarization — both as those connections operated inside their conscientious objector organization and within contemporary Turkish society as a whole. They generously asked me to join one of their lively dinner conversations. It was out of conversations such as these that Ferda and other Turkish women later crafted their own "*I Reject...*" declaration.

Stories. These three stories remind me that this is how a new consciousness comes about. In this instance, my own. While women within conscientious objection movements can appear as a collective phenomenon, their experiences and the new curiosities, new investigations, and new awarenesses often are best understood by telling stories. So, as we read the eye-opening chapters that follow, it will help, I think, not to lose sight of the stories of individual women — in Colombia, Eritrea, Israel, Korea, Turkey, Britain, the USA and Paraguay — crafting a new politics out of telling and reflecting upon their own particular stories. Out of a convergence of stories comes a movement. Out of a reflection on the messiness of women's individual stories, their twists and turns, their surprises, their loose ends, comes a movement that is sustainable and vibrant in its challenging patriarchy's sneaky ways of infecting both militarism and efforts to challenge militarism.

Cynthia Enloe is professor in the Department of International Development, Community, and Environment at Clark University, Worcester, USA, and Director of Clark University's Women Studies program. She is the author of many books on feminism and militarism, among them: Bananas, Beaches and Bases. Making Feminist Sense of International Politics, *London, Sidney, Wellington, Pandora, 1989, and* Maneuvers: The International Politics of Militarizing Women's Lives, *University of California Press, 2000.*

Introduction

By Ellen Elster and Majken Jul Sørensen, War Resisters' International

Why this Anthology

Many women have been active in peace work, both in women-only groups and in mixed movements. There are still many stories to be told about their experiences. Very little, if any at all, attention has been given to the women who have become conscientious objectors as a protest against militarism in both wartime and peacetime, in many different places in the world. *War Resisters' International* (WRI) decided to publish this book in order to give the women who declare themselves conscientious objectors a voice. Most of the texts in this book are written by women who have made a public declaration of conscientious objection or otherwise supported male conscientious objectors. "Public" should here be understood in a broad sense including statements made in courts, and letters to the authorities. Although the book can be read as a contribution to the debate on conscription for women, we would like to stress that it is a book about conscientious objection as resistance to militarism, not about resistance to conscription itself.

Most of the articles in this volume have been written especially for this book. A few of the contributions have been published before in the WRI publication *The Broken Rifle* or in other peace movement magazines — this is particularly the case for declarations and for material about the past. We have not tried to highlight all the cases of women's conscientious objection in wartime. What we have tried to offer is an anthology which can illustrate the diversity among women conscientious objectors as to time (wartime or peacetime) and geography. WRI saw a need to collect these stories in order to show the span that these women cover in their working methods, their reasons for becoming conscientious objectors, and the challenges they face. This representation is yet another way of campaigning against militarism.

Some of the contributors were actually facing conscription; others had joined the military "voluntarily" and then developed their conscientious objection during military service. We also have a contribution from Korea reflecting on the role women have played in the movement for conscientious objection there without making any declarations themselves.

Through the years much has been written about women's actions and campaigns for peace and against war and militarism. In modern times, the birth of the *Women's International League for Peace and Freedom*, when women from different parts of the world met in The Hague in 1915 to protest against the war and to find ways out of it [1], is a powerful showing of women's strength against militarism. The experiences of women who faced military service directly through conscription during World War II have been less documented. With the women's liberation movement from the beginning of the 1970s, much literature has appeared on women, militarism and feminism, women and war, victimisation of women during wars, women as soldiers. The years from 1970 to 1980 explored women's actions against militarism [2], including marches, organisations such as *Women for Peace*, women's peace camps of which *Greenham Common* was only one among many, creative nonviolent actions like the *Women's Pentagon Action*, and *Shibokusa women* of Kita Fuji.

Towards the end of 1980 women expanded their actions by crossing the border and shaking hands with their sisters on the other side. *Women in Black* [3] appeared for the first time in December 1988 in Jerusalem as vigils consisting of Israeli and Palestinian women proclaimed the message of "ending occupation". The idea was picked up by Italian feminists, who again inspired women in Belgrade in the early 1990's, where women gathered in silent protest every Wednesday against the war then being conducted and actively reached out to women in other parts of the former Yugoslavia. The idea spread worldwide. Through the network in the WRI, we see that women opposing militarism outside of Western Europe and North and South America have a more holistic approach to antimilitarism, and also include social empowerment and resistance to poverty and different forms of oppression and patriarchal structures [4]. *Cynthia Cockburn* [5], in her research of women against war and militarism around the world, has found that patriarchy is an important factor of militarism. For this reason, women sometimes prefer to organise as women. They need the room to voice women's specific experience of war and women's particular capacity and skills in surviving war and building peace.

When we set out to collect material for this anthology, we knew that we wanted to explore the theme of women's conscientious objection to both military service and to militarism. But we were not sure where to draw the line between *"women's conscientious objection to militarism"* and all the other peace work that women participate in. War Resisters' International has for a long time had an understanding of conscientious objection as something much more than objection to obligatory military service, without being clear about where conscientious objection ends, and other peace work begins. We don't think there is a definite answer to this question, but in the final chapter we will clarify what we mean when we talk about conscientious objection in both the broad and narrow sense.

The Contributions to the Anthology

In her contribution, *Ferda Ülker* from Turkey points to the fact that, most frequently, people consider conscientious objection as having to do only with men and their refusal to serve in the military, and this is something we find in several of the other contributions. However, we want to make it absolutely clear that our understanding of conscientious objection reaches far beyond the legal understanding of the concept as practised by military authorities around the world. Conscientious objection is something that concerns us all, no matter whether we are conscripted or not and no matter whether we are men or women.

In Turkey, where women are not conscripted, the priority of the conscientious objection movement has been to support men who are in prison. But as *Ferda Ülker* writes, the reason why women are not conscripted is not because they have gained a right they have been fighting for. They don't have to serve because the military leaders don't consider them worthy of doing this *"glorious duty"*. But the women in Turkey who have declared themselves conscientious objectors (12 at the time of her writing) give many different reasons why they find it necessary to declare themselves as such.

The French women who in 1991 declared themselves conscientious objectors are using arguments similar to the Turkish women. They connect the army with patriarchy and hierarchy and refuse to support the militarisation of society. Only they among the contributors use arguments that reach out of their own society and connect militarism with sexual abuse happening in societies around the world where there are military bases.

Most people can understand why pacifist men facing conscription become conscientious objectors, even if they don't agree with them. But women's declarations do not receive the same understanding in Turkey, where they are considered incomprehensible and unnecessary since women are not conscripted. However, because people question women's declarations, it also opens discussion in a different way from men's declarations. In this way, the incomprehensibility becomes a *"window of opportunity"* for discussions about militarism.

Hilal Demir, also from Turkey, continues along the same line as *Ferda Ülker*. She explains how the independent group *"Antimilitarist feminists"* was organised by a group of women who had been active in the *Izmir War Resisters' Association*. She wrote her own declaration in 2005, motivated to prevent patriarchy from *"leaking into our movement"*, arguing that fighting militarism is more than fighting military service. Within the antimilitarist movement in Turkey, the women who have declared themselves conscientious objectors have been criticised by other women, who feel that the use of the term *"conscientious objection"* plays into the hands of the military by acknowledging their rules. In *Hilal Demir*'s opinion, adopting the conscientious objection platform has proved useful, since it has helped bring attention to the situation of the women within the antimilitarist movement in a way that has never happened before. In addition, the declarations have encouraged the search for new perspectives on women's antimilitarist activism.

On the other side of the globe, in Paraguay and Colombia, we find many parallels to Turkey. Both Paraguay and Colombia are militarised societies with no compulsory conscription for women. Colombia is still torn by a civil war that has been going on for more than 40 years. However, in these two countries a number of women have decided to declare themselves conscientious objectors, arguing that a militaristic society affects not just men, but everyone. They are frequently questioned as to why they as women declare themselves objectors when they are not forced to do military service. Their answer is that they are objecting to the prevailing culture of militarism that is affecting all aspects of life, the machismo culture which has deep roots in militarism, as well as the patriarchy which is upheld by the current power structures. The women in the conscientious objection movement in Paraguay have made a conscious decision to work in the same organisation as men, arguing that it is important to discuss the subject of feminism and militarism together with men.

In a joint declaration in 2002, the Paraguayan women argue that they object in conscience to the military as a system of economic, social and cultural oppression. We find almost the same expression in the declaration that Milena Romero Sanabaria from Colombia made. The Paraguayans also argue that the recent practice of letting women into the military is used as a justification for an increase in the military budget. Several of the Colombian declarations stress the objection to patriarchy, and the importance of declaring oneself a conscientious objector as an individual act.

In her article about conscientious objection in Colombia, *Andrea Ochoa* explains that the women decided to declare themselves conscientious objectors not just as an act of solidarity with men who become conscientious objectors, but in order to promote peace and nonviolence to a wider public. She explains that the work on conscientious objection has especially spread to children and young people through the use of alternative pedagogy. The guerillas and the paramilitaries recruit women into their service (both voluntarily and forcefully) in the name of gender equality. This is one reason why Colombian women have found it useful to declare themselves conscientious objectors. In addition it has been a way to create public discussions about alternatives to the war, and to give women an equal position to men in the conscientious objection movement.

At the time of writing, there are two countries in the world that conscript women, Israel and Eritrea. Both have recently been involved in wars, and both of them have introduced military service for women in the name of gender equality. But there are also many differences. In Eritrea, there is no recognition of conscientious objection at all, forcing all objectors to flee the country. We include the stories of two of these women. *Ruta Yosef-Tudla* is against war on principle, and managed to flee Eritrea before she was forced into the military. *Bisrat Habte Micael* tells about the terrible conditions, including sexual abuses, that she and other women have experienced in the military.

In Israel, pacifists can obtain exemption from military service because of their beliefs and, although marginalised, conscientious objectors raise a voice in the public debate. *Idan Halili* and *Tali Lerner* give us an introduction to women's considerations about conscription and refusal in Israel. *Idan Halili* describes her own refusal on feminist grounds, and we follow the transformation she goes through within a short period of time from a girl who wants to use the military as a place to work for equal rights, to a woman using feminism as her argument for becoming a conscientious objector. She was the first woman in Israel to apply to the so-called conscientious committee for an exemption from military service because she is a feminist. At that time she did not consider herself a pacifist, but she refused to participate in all armies because they conflicted with her feminist values. As *Idan Halili* says, an army which is nonviolent, non-aggressive and non-hierarchical would not be an army.

Both *Idan Halili* and *Tali Lerner* point out that this understanding of feminism is far removed from the usual perception of feminism in Israel. From the mainstream perspective, feminists are the women who become fighter pilots. They both argue that these women are only accepted into these positions when they adopt masculine identities.

Tali Lerner gives us a glimpse of how militarised Israeli society is, and how closely military service is connected to citizenship. Many marginalised groups like Bedouins and homosexuals use military service as their *"entry ticket"* into society. She also describes how it has recently become more difficult for women to get an exemption from military service, since women objectors are now facing the same hard conditions that male objectors have experienced over the years.

From the United States *Stephanie Atkinson* and *Diedra Cobb* give us their personal stories of how they got recruited into the military, and how they developed their refusal. Both of them realised that something was not quite right soon after their entry into the military, but getting out of the US military is much more difficult than joining it. Although *Stephanie Atkinson* points out very clearly that she does not consider herself a conscientious objector, she left the service for reasons of conscience by going absent without leave (AWOL). We also present three short statements from three other American women, *Tina Garnaez, Anita Cole* and *Katherine Jashinski*. *Tina Garnaez* points out that military recruiters in US high schools especially target minority students who see the military as the only way out of poverty. They also recruit aggressively among the working class, religious groups, agrarian and conservative communities. *Stephanie Atkinson* tells us that she speaks on behalf of young people who have no direction in life and limited economic opportunity, who experience emotional problems and who are in homes with a single parent or with stepfathers or stepmothers. The five women's paths to conscientious objection are very personal. *Anita Cole* joined the military because she wanted to serve her country and not for economic reasons. Her refusal developed over time, but the turning point was when she was urged on during weapons practice by an officer saying, *"Come on, you're a killer"*.

Female conscientious objectors actually faced conscription in Britain during Word War II. This story is told by *Mitzi Bales*. Some of these women were called "absolutists", what we today would call total objectors, since they refused to accept alternative service as well. *Kathleen Lonsdale* was a Quaker and well-known scientist, who did not even have to register for service since she had three children under 14 years old. But she decided to register in order to be able to refuse. There are probably as many reasons for refusal as there are women who refused, but from the papers and interviews that are available today, we do not get the impression of feminist reasons for refusal that we find many years later in Israel. *Nora Page* gave as her reason that she did not want to do anything in wartime that she would not be asked to do in peacetime. Joan Williams chose a different path from the absolutists and refused to register at all. Some of these women conscientious objectors were fined or imprisoned repeatedly, a tactic also frequently used today, for example, in Turkey (for men) and in Israel.

In the US during Word War II, women also refused to participate in the war effort, and supported the men who became conscientious objectors. *Erna Harris* tells about the different kind of tasks she would do to support the men who were in camps. Whereas the British women were facing demands to register and be appointed to work to support the war effort, women in the US were facing less direct demands. However, women who refused to perform duties they associated with supporting the war effort risked losing their job, something which happened to *Jean Zwickel* when she refused to help register soldiers.

Using a case from Sweden, we also introduce the theme of refusing compulsory civil defence duties that do not involve carrying arms or participating in combat training. *Majken Jul Sørensen* writes about *Barbro Alving*, who served a one-month prison sentence in 1956 for refusing her obligatory civil defence training. Her refusal was a reaction to the madness of a possible nuclear war, and the authorities' *"double speak"* on the issue. She grounded her refusal in both feminism and a radical pacifist stand which she developed when she participated in a big campaign against civil defence training as a young woman in 1935. Refusal to perform civil defence duties is a subject that deserves more attention.

We find a similar sort of resistance in Germany in the late 1970s. For over a decade, women had been "offered" the opportunity of receiving nursing training with the enticement that it would help them get jobs in hospitals in peacetime. Over the years there was a growing awareness that the training was intended as a preparation for war, and linked to the military system. Women who participated in the training started to send letters protesting against this link and indicating that they would refuse wartime service.

In the statement *"Total Resistance to Military Service"* from 1980, women who signed this statement argue that feminists need to resist not just conscription, but also alternative service. They echo the British absolutists from WWII and *Barbro Alving* from Sweden when they write: "*Recognition of an alternative service implies the recognition of the structure and purpose of the military...*". It is the same argument made 25 years later by Turkish women conscientious objectors. This statement uses a line of argument for women's conscientious objection grounded in feminism. It clearly illustrates the broad definition of conscientious objection which is the focus of this book. The women are making a clear condemnation of militarism from a feminist perspective of rejecting patriarchy and refusing to be part of a system which is oppressively damaging to women.

In order to explore all aspects of women's conscientious objection, we have also included an example where the term is used in its traditional narrow sense. In 1985 in Belgium, women demanded that everybody who shares the philosophy of conscientious objection should also have the right to the status. Their argument was that male conscientious objectors had the right not to accept work in the defence industry, a right that was denied to women. This case is a clear example of the old argument that *"we want the same rights as men"*. It also makes this case differently from most of the other stories in this book. The Belgian women were aware that, by demanding a right for conscientious objection status, they indirectly support the system of conscription and alternative service. However, they still argue that it is important for women to have the same rights as men.

We hope that this anthology will be interesting for both men and women as an illustration of how militarism affects both sexes. We also hope that it will inspire activism and encourage more women to become conscientious objectors and more men to support them. We believe that the broader peace movement will find the reflections on how conscientious objection can be used as a challenge to militarism informative and thought provoking. Finally, we hope it can be useful for feminists who are not at the moment concerned with antimilitarism, to see how closely feminism and antimilitarism are linked.

Footnotes

[1] Bussey & Tims: *Pioneers for Peace. Women's International League for Peace and Freedom 1915–1965.* WILPF 1980. Anne Wiltsher: *Most Dangerous Women. Feminist Peace campaigners of the great war.* Pandora 1985. Jill Liddington: *The long road to Greenham. Feminism and anti-militarism in Britain since 1820.* Virago Press 1989.
[2] Lynne Jones (ed): *Keeping the Peace. A Women's Peace Handbook.* The Women's Press 1983. Cook & Kirk: *Greenham Women Everywhere. Dreams, Ideas and Actions from the Women's Peace Movement.* Pluto Press 1983. Pam McAllister (ed): *Reweaving the Web of Life. Feminism and Nonviolence.* New Society Publishers 1982.
[3] Living reconciliation – Making Peace. Women's strategies against oppression, war and armament. *International Women's Congress in Nürnberg 1992.* Women for Peace. Women in Black, Belgrade 1997. Cynthia Cockburn: *From Where We Stand: War, Women's Activism and Feminist Analysis.* Zed Books 2007.
[4] Raj & Roy Choudhury (ed): *Contemporary Social Movements in India: Achievements and Hurdles.* Indian Social Institute 1998.
[5] Cynthia Cockburn: *From Where We Stand: War, Women's Activism and Feminist Analysis.* Zed Books 2007.

Marie Marcks donated this drawing to the WRI Women's Working Group for the promotion of WRI's 4th International Women's Conference "Women Overcoming Violence — Redefining Development and Changing Society Through Nonviolence" in Bangkok, Thailand, in November 1992

They said "No" to War:

British Women Conscientious Objectors in World War II

By Mitzi Bales, peace activist and member of War Resisters' International

As *Nora Page* was driven off to prison in the Black Maria on 15 January 1943, she said to herself: "*I must carry it through*". Nora Page was not the first young British woman to declare herself a conscientious objector. Nor was she the first to be imprisoned for her stand. But her story is left to us in a lengthy interview recorded at the Imperial War Museum in 1980. She expressed her beliefs as strongly as ever. After all, she had been a member of the *Peace Pledge Union* (PPU) since 1937 and volunteered as an adviser to conscientious objectors from 1941 to 1945.

Her story tells us how conscription during World War II affected women who said *"No"* to war as a matter of conscientious belief. It also gives us some insights into how conscientious objection was viewed by the wider society.

During the years of growing unease with Hitler's dictatorship and military conquests, there was also a developing peace movement. Nora came across a street corner vendor of *Peace News* (PN), the publication of the PPU, and read about the organisation. It was not long before she herself joined the PPU and was actively selling *Peace News*.

The anti-conscription movement developed in 1939 as part of the peace movement. Nora became interested when she saw a newspaper notice about a meeting on the subject. She was impressed that the founder of the movement was not a pacifist, but was against conscription. When conscription came, she joined small pickets leafleting Employment Exchanges, where those liable to conscription had to register, with information about the possibility of conscientious objection.

Nora explained that, for the most part, the public had an indulgent "*couldn't care less*" attitude to peace activists until the war actually started. There was some harassment by police, who made PN vendors and leafletters move on if several passers-by gathered for a chat at the same time. However, she and her comrades managed in general to keep good relations with both the public and the police in her area of London. She developed a good technique of disarming the few hecklers by answering them with a new bit of information.

With the limited extension of military conscription to women in 1941, and the tightening up of industrial conscription and compulsory firewatching for both men and women, Nora's story became that of a conscientious objector. There was a particular problem in that, although there was provision for claiming conscientious objection to military service, there was no legal right of conscientious objection to industrial or firewatching compulsion. Nora's road to imprisonment provides one example of women conscientious objectors in World War II.

First, Nora was given "direction of labour", as the law put it, to work in a greengrocer's shop. As an "absolutist" — the term adopted by conscientious objectors who would not accept any work releasing someone for military service — she refused the order. Nora did not disparage the assigned work, declaring in her interview, *"My attitude was not to be directed to do anything in wartime that you wouldn't have asked me to do in peacetime"*. It seems that, unusually, no further action was taken — the Ministry of Labour and National Service had so many people to chase up for the *"war effort"* that some just got away.

However, as she says, she was caught by another regulation: *"I was in a firewatch team in our road and I took my turn stopping up all night. Then we were directed to register for firewatching... I wrote and told them I had not registered because I did not believe in conscription"*. She had to appear at the magistrates' court in Tottenham, north London, and was sentenced to 14 days in Holloway prison for women.

After being taken down to the cells, she and the others under sentence were allowed to receive lunch from some women who had attended the court. She says that the women jailers were helpful and actually waved them off as they departed in the Black Maria. In this, Nora's experience varies greatly from many other women conscientious objectors, who were humiliated and verbally abused during their hearings and afterwards.

Other industrial and firewatching conscientious objectors

Nora served her 14 days at the same time as *Kathleen Lonsdale*, the eminent Quaker scientist, who was also serving a month for refusing firewatching registration. They never met, but Nora says that it was *"nice to know someone with a big name"* was in prison with her.

Kathleen Lonsdale was a crystallographer who developed several X-ray techniques. This work, plus other contributions to chemistry and physics, later earned her a Fellowship of the Royal Society. As a married mother of three children under 14, she was exempt from registration, but she chose to refuse on conscientious principle, and became the first Quaker woman to be jailed as a conscientious objector. She declared that she had no objection to firewatching, but felt that the issue of the war itself and the infringement of civil liberties inherent in compulsion were more important.

While in Holloway, Kathleen held a Quaker meeting every week, protested to improve the poor conditions, and generally helped to keep up the morale of the other prisoners in her block. After her release she wrote a memoir of prison life, one of the few to come out of that period. Published by the Prison Medical Reform Council, it is valuable as a factual record of the deprivations experienced by prisoners, though there is an emphasis on medical issues.

Turning to the very first woman imprisoned as a conscientious objector, in January 1942, we meet *Connie Bolam*, a parlour maid to *Kitty Alexander*, herself one of a whole family of conscientious objectors, in Newcastle, northern England. Connie was directed to do land, canteen or hospital work. Another firm absolutist, she refused, and was sentenced to a month in prison by Newcastle magistrates, and went to Durham Gaol. In June the same year she appeared before the Northumberlnnd and Durham Tribunal as a conscientious objector to military conscription, where the Chairman was hostile, saying, *"We on the tribunal have some commonsense and you have none. It is no good talking rubbish to us like that"*. She was allowed exemption conditional upon doing farm, hospital or canteen work, against which she unsuccessfully appealed for unconditional exemption, and seems finally to have accepted the conditional exemption. She may have had other matters in mind: she received numerous letters arising from publicity around her case, and married one of her well-wishers. *Kitty Alexander*, meanwhile, had also refused to register for employment, and was imprisoned for a month, as well as being dismissed from her job in an insurance office.

Ivy Watson, too, had a gruelling experience. Having refused to register for employment, she appeared before the magistrates at Stratford (east London) three days before Christmas 1943. She was ordered to pay a £25 fine or face three months in prison. She chose prison, but after four weeks her health was so impaired that she asked her family to pay the balance of the fine so she could be released.

Her account in the CBCO Bulletin tallies with *Kathleen Lonsdale*'s memoir. She tells how the prisoners had only one small cake of soap per month, one pair of stockings, no handkerchief, no coat, no toilet paper. Like others, she used a dirty blanket as a wrap against the severe cold and tore up the bible, the only source of paper, for toilet wipes. She also suffered mental torture. She had asked for the Free Church minister to visit her, and he came on the appointed day. But the prison authorities told him that she didn't want to see him and he went away in bewilderment. This seemed to be the blow she couldn't cope with.

Joan Williams (née Locke) was an assistant in Shoreditch public library who left a chronicle entitled *Experiences of a Woman CO 1939-43*. She was required to register in August 1941 along with all those in her age group, then 26. She refused, and wrote to the Minister of Labour saying so. She had an acknowledgement of her letter, but heard no further till June 1942. Then she was again called to register and again she refused. There was correspondence to and fro till March 1943 when she received a summons to attend Clerkenwell Magistrates' Court, on a prosecution for refusing a direction. On her continued refusal, she was remanded for two weeks and told to think over her decision. She held to it, however, and at the renewed hearing her exchange with the magistrates gave an interesting perspective on how conscientious objectors defended themselves:

Joan W: I recognise that the country has been very generous in its treatment of conscientious objectors, but there is no conscientious clause in the industrial conscription act. It is to the principle of the act that I object.
Magistrate: You object to the law?
Joan W: Because it is the organisation of the country for war purposes, and I feel I cannot take part in it.
Magistrate: Do you refuse to have the direction? Otherwise you will have to go to prison.
Joan W: I would rather go to prison.

She was sentenced to two months, later commuted to six weeks. Her account relates her time at Holloway. She tells us that there were three or four Jehovah's Witnesses, one Methodist, one person of no denomination, and one Quaker among the conscientious objectors she met on arriving at the prison. They were able to meet and talk a little during exercise periods and Quaker visitors came to see them. Joan worked in the library, cleaning floors, taking books round and typing a book catalogue. After her release she received three more notices to be interviewed, but nothing came of it.

Like *Joan Williams*, other women refused even to register for directions of labour. They were fined or sent to prison, sometimes more than once. Statistics published in 1948 give the following details.

M M Day: 1942: £8 fine or 2 months' imprisonment. Fine paid. Again, 28 days and 3 months concurrent.
Margaret Prendergast, Liverpool: 1941, £3 fine, never collected. 1942, Tribunal, 1943, 1 month in prison.
Betty Brown, Scunthorpe, Lincs: 1942, £5 fine or 28 days' imprisonment, served. 1944, £10 fine or 1 month, served.
J Fermer: 1944, £5 fine, paid anonymously. Again, £10 fine or 1 month.

Although these cold figures do not reveal the human side of these women's stories, the reason for the repeated fines or threats of imprisonment is that each refusal of compliance was, in law, a new offence. The real mischief was the failure of the state to recognise conscientious objection to industrial conscription.

Women conscientious objectors to military service

Britain was first among the World War II Allies to conscript women into wartime forces and, therefore, the first country to produce women conscientious objectors. On 18 December 1941 Parliament passed a law making all single women between the ages of 19 and 31 potentially liable for service in the Woman's Royal Naval Service, the Auxiliary Territorial Service, the Women's Auxiliary Air Force or Civil Defence, but none would be required to use a lethal weapon. The conscientious objection provisions for men were carried over to these women in identical terms.

The women's cause was also immediately taken up by the Central Board for Conscientious Objectors (CBCO, chaired by *Fenner Brockway*, former imprisoned World War I conscientious objector, and former Chair of the [British] *No More War Movement* and the WRI, though by World War II no longer a pacifist), which had been founded in 1939 by a number of peace organisations to help all conscientious objectors. The CBCO represented objectors in many ways, in particular advising on registration, tribunal and court procedures, and lobbying parliament and government on their behalf.

Although the 1941 act permitted call-up of women aged 19-31, the provision was in fact exercised only for women aged up to 24. Women in this group were first called to interview, and those already in professions such as teaching, nursing, or working on the land, or women offering immediately to take up such work, were usually dismissed and did not need to formally register as conscientious objectors, but they could if they wished. Other women became liable to call-up, unless they obtained some kind of exemption, including conscientious objection.

Women registering as conscientious objectors did so initially at an Employment Exchange, and then submitted a statement of their objection to a Local Tribunal, where they could attend a hearing to adjudicate upon their application. Local Tribunals comprised a legally qualified chair plus four members appointed by the Minister of Labour; of these, one at least had to be a trade unionist and one a woman. In the case of a woman applicant the Tribunal could make one of three findings: to register the woman unconditionally as a conscientious objector; to register her as a conscientious objector upon specified conditions (for example work in teaching, nursing, on the land, or civil defence); or to remove her from the conscientious objector register, that is, reject her application.

If the conscientious objector disagreed with the Local Tribunal finding, she could appeal to the Appellate Tribunal. Of 1000 women who appeared before Local Tribunals, about half appealed. It is interesting that a greater proportion of women than men took this step. This was due to the large number of appeals by absolutists who wanted to make a formal stand; many women in a position equivalent to men accepting conditional exemption did not appear in the conscientious objection statistics at all because of the initial informal interview procedure already described.

Some Local Tribunals seemed to dislike women objectors. At the hearing of *Hazel Kerr*, for example, one tribunal member chided that if Hazel carried her argument to its logical conclusion, she should eat nothing and starve herself to death. *"That might be the most useful thing to do"*. Twenty members of the public walked out in protest. It was at the same hearing that the previously cited remark was made to *Connie Bolam*.

Highlights

The first woman conscientious objector was formally recognised by a Tribunal on 2 April 1942. She was *Joyce Allen*, aged 21, a member of East Horndon PPU. She was exempted on condition of her remaining in teaching, and accepted this, although towards the end of the war she transferred to the Friends Relief Service in Liverpool. Later in life she was active in the radical anti-nuclear war movement and the green movement, and was interviewed as a former conscientious objector by the *Guardian* in 2005.

In the two weeks following Joyce's tribunal, *M E Wells* of Scarborough and *Alma Gillinder* of Swalwell-on-Tyne were registered conditional upon nursing or hospital work.

On 16 April, three more women were registered conditionally. Two were Jehovah's Witnesses, who accepted hospital work, and the third agreed to work full time in her father's bakery or on the land.

Marjorie Whittles, of Liverpool, was the first woman conscientious objector to be registered unconditionally, on 20 April 1942. She joined the Friends Ambulance Unit, and later transferred to the Friends War Relief Service. Later still, she married another conscientious objector, *Michael Asquith*, a grandson of *Herbert Asquith*, the Prime Minister who first introduced British conscription in 1916 (with recognition of conscientious objection).

On 21 March 1944, 27-year-old *Rita Matthews* of the Isle of Wight, a Jehovah's Witness, was sentenced by a magistrates' court to 12 months' imprisonment for non-compliance with the conditions of her exemption (nursing or other hospital work). This was reduced to six months on appeal to the Quarter Sessions, the Ministry of Labour bearing her appeal costs.

Untold stories

It has been 69 years since Britain enacted conscription for women in 1941. The time gap means that research into the subject is ever more difficult. The youngest surviving conscientious objectors are now in their eighties and hard to find. There were 37 years between *Nora Page*'s experience as a conscientious objector and the Imperial War Museum interview that preserved her words for later generations. Fortunately, eleven more women conscientious objectors, including *Marjorie Whittles*, were recorded, but clearly there are hundreds of untold stories.

The figures are complicated. The total number of women who appeared before tribunals is given as 1,056 (including 59 prosecuted for non-compliance with conditions), but the figure obviously does not include women who accepted an informal assignment to non-military work, but who in other circumstances would probably have demanded recognition as conscientious objectors. The figures arising from industrial conscription and compulsory firewatching, are even more difficult, but there were 430 known prosecutions of women for conscientious objection offences in these areas. If these figures seem tiny in comparison with 60,000 men objectors in World War II, it is because a much smaller proportion of women became liable for any kind of compulsion, and over a significantly shorter period.

In any assessment of women in the British conscientious objection movement, their part other than as conscientious objectors must not be overlooked. *Nancy Browne*, first secretary of CBCO, was the human contact welcomed by all conscientious objectors turning to the Board for help. *Myrtle Solomon*, the last secretary, combining it with the General Secretaryship of the PPU, and then Chair of the WRI, was a human contact for conscientious objectors in difficulty in many parts of the world. Nor should we forget their precursors in World War I, *Catherine Marshall, Joan Beauchamp* and *Margaret Hobhouse*. As to the present and future, it should be remembered that the current right to request a discharge from the British armed forces on grounds of conscientious objection applies to women equally with men, though no case is known so far of a woman seeking such a discharge.

Unknown women conscientious objectors carried the banner for peace in their time, along with the women whose names and stories are known. They can all be acknowledged in our thoughts for their strength of purpose and principled stand against war.

References
Barker, Rachel: Conscience, Government and War, Routledge & Kegan Paul, 1982
Benjamin, Alison: Voices of Reason, Guardian, 3 August 2005
Central Board for Conscientious Objectors (CBCO): Records, Friends' House Library
Hayes, Denis: Challenge of Conscience, published for CBCO by George Allen & Unwin 1949
Imperial War Museum: Sound Archive, Conscientious Objectors
Lonsdale, Kathleen: Prison for Women, Prison Medical Reform Council, 1943
Peace Pledge Union: Database of British COs, including 150 women
Williams, Joan: Experiences of a Woman CO 1939–43, unpublished manuscript, Friends' House Library

US Women Conscientious Objectors in World War II

When *Woodrow Wilson* introduced the Selective Service Act [1] in 1917 in the United States, it included all men 21 to 30 years of age. Popularly this has been known as conscription or the draft. There was massive resistance by labour, pacifist and progressive groups. Thousands were jailed and some tortured. The patriotic fever and the repression of groups opposing the war caused a major split in American society.

When *Franklin Roosevelt* reintroduced the Selective Service Act of 1940, this act included men between the ages of 18 and 45 years. The law included the Right of Conscientious Objection for religious groups. Conscientious Objectors had to participate as non-combatants to serve the war effort. Some were taken to Civilian Public Service (CPS) camps [2] throughout the country to do various projects like work in mental hospitals, fight forest fires, and other services the government felt important. Many pacifists and other religious and non-religious objectors began to see these camps as concentration camps. Others felt they wanted no part of the war effort in their goal of ending all war. A movement among people in conscientious objector camps started when people left the camps and risked arrest. Some were tracked down and put on trial and went to prison. Most sentences were harsh and resisters suffered isolation and intimidation by prison staff and inmates alike.

Women in this era, as in the past and the present, were not subject to the selective service laws. Women could join as noncombatants in the war effort voluntarily. Many joined the military in this way. Some served the war effort by working in factories and jobs related to the war because there was a need for a total war effort. Although women were not required by law to "serve", there was tremendous societal pressure to support and not question the war. Before the war was declared there was a huge peace movement of pacifists, isolationists, communists and socialists. Men and women throughout the country were in these movements. When the war broke out most eligible men were drafted into the military or sent to Civilian Public Service (CPS) — or Conscientious Objector — camps, or prison for resisting. Women were left in charge of the pacifist organizations throughout the country. They supported the men in the CPS camps and in prison. They ran the pacifist organizations such as the *War Resisters League* and the *Fellowship of Reconciliation*. They found rooms for conscientious objectors to sleep when they walked out of the CPS camps, which was breaking the law because they were harboring criminals. Many women organized and attended anti-war demonstrations and meetings. Other women attended trials of conscientious objectors who left the CPS camps and later visited them in prison when they were found guilty. Women were conscientious objectors in thought and action.

Jean Zwickel

Jean Zwickel moved to the Harlem Ashram in New York city after she was fired for refusing to conscript students during World War II. Married to Jewish CO *Abe Zwickel*, they remained active in the peace movement into their eighties. Here is her story:

I was finishing my second year of teaching when the war broke. The teachers were asked to help with registration of soldiers. I talked to the superintendent and said I didn't want to participate or cooperate with the war. I was not propagandizing in my classes against it but just didn't want any participation. He said that would be perfectly all right. There was a second call to the teachers to help with conscription. This was a little more urgent and a little more compulsory. Teachers were really expected to do their share. I did consent to help with the rationing of the gas, but registration I couldn't see. So when it came time to renew contracts I found I was out of a job. The excuse they gave me was that classes in German and French would be going down. I wouldn't be needed. But I'm sure the main cause was my opposition to the war.

Erna Harris

Erna Harris was a Black journalist who became active with pacifist and civil rights movements in Los Angeles, California, during World War II.

I was part of the War Resisters League and the Fellowship of Reconciliation. I was a member, and I was there. We didn't formalize it as a support group, but I was there taking my chances for going to prison ... encouraging violation of the Selective Service Act and later when the guys were in the camp and some of them went over the hill [3] from camps. A lot of them spent several nights on the floor in my living room in the apartment I rented with Ella, a German girlfriend. She and I had a little apartment and I would move out of my room and sleep back in her room so the COs could sleep on the floor in my room. They didn't have any money and we were harboring criminals.

What we women were mostly doing was trying to take care of the guys who went to camp and make sure they didn't feel deserted, which was easy to feel, and to take care of the ones who didn't get their classification or who decided not to register [4] and, therefore, were in trials or on their way to prisons. I went to trails more than enough, and tried to be known to authorities as being part of this business because I didn't see any reason those guys should suffer more than the women. Women were raising money for bond [5], keeping in touch, being runners to check for bail bond to get the guys out, pulling cases together, stuff like that. Keep lawyers working. The ones that typed well, typed for the boys. I visited the camps, but I didn't come to pray with them or bring them cookies. I would commiserate and tell them we were trying to stop the war back there. So I probably was more welcome than a lot of others. Cookies and visits and people praying for them were nice, but what they needed was somebody to roust the government.

The stories of Jean Zwickel and Erna Harris are from "Against the Tide: Pacifist Resistance in the Second World War", an Oral History edited by Deena Hurwitz and Craig Simpson. The 1984 War Resisters League Calendar.

Introduction and footnotes by Joanne Sheehan and Craig Simpson

Footnotes

[1] Selective Service Act: The US Government conscription law.
[2] Civilian Public Service camp: where conscientious objectors did alternative service.
[3] Went over the hill: escaping from the camps, where they felt they were voluntarily submitting to their own imprisonment.
[4] Didn't get their classification or who decided not to register: men in World War II and today are required by law to register for Selective Service. Some received a classification of "Conscientious Objector". If they didn't get the CO status or they didn't register at all, they were subject to arrest and imprisonment.
[5] Bond/Bail Bond: Money that a person arrested needs to pay in order to get out of gaol before a trial.

Swedish Women's Civil Defence Refusal 1935–1956

By Majken Jul Sørensen, War Resisters' International

At the beginning of 1956, a woman called *Barbro Alving* spent one month in prison for refusing to participate in civil defence training. Under the pen name "Bang", she was a well known writer and journalist, and, among many other things, she had reported directly on the Spanish civil war for one of the major Swedish newspapers. The prison sentence was the end of a long process. *Barbro Alving* had made her initial refusal to participate in air raid defence training four years earlier in 1952. She experienced a couple of police interrogations before the verdict was handed down at the end of 1954.[1]

In her speech to the court in Stockholm which decided on her case, she said:

> There are times in life when an action which apparently looks negative — a no — can be positive. The civil defence duty places me in such a situation as a woman, and as a pacifist. No one who is present here can influence the least what happens in Washington and Moscow, in London and Peking [Beijing]. You can only be responsible for what you do with your own life. I have found that the only action my conscience commands me to do is to contribute to the **wintering of the thought**, which in spite of everything, is to be found in millions of men and women: that you should refuse to participate in anything which goes against all reason and can indicate suicide of humanity [2].

Her refusal took place in the context of the public's growing knowledge about the devastating consequences of nuclear war in the aftermath of World War II, and the threat of a third world war, which is the *"suicide of humanity"* she refers to. In an article about civil defence that she wrote in 1955 [3], her arguments against civil defence duties is focus on the madness of nuclear war, and the lack of coherence in the authorities' arguments about war and defence.

She explains that the obligatory enrolment of women in the civil defence forces is proof that a modern military system cannot function without active contribution from women. War has become total, and so has "defence". Women therefore have a responsibility to search their consciences for the right thing to do as a reaction to an absurd system which goes against all reason. When the scenario for the authorities is total war, her answer is total objection. She refuses to take part in any kind of training which is connected to the military system and the logic of total war and total defence.

Some of the criticism directed against her claimed that, by refusing to learn basic medical care, she was refusing to help victims of war. As a response, she wrote:

"There is another set of questions one as a civil defence objector is faced with. Just [think] about this: What would you do if the war comes. Will you stand with your arms crossed then? What will you do if a bleeding person stumbles in front of your feet?

Help, you say.

But isn't it better to practise ahead of time so that one can help more efficiently? Said with a certain eager triumph.

No, you answer.

That is a question about two different things, two different situations (...) **During peace time one still has the freedom to choose what you want to fight for** (...) With all the power you have at your disposal, you fight against what your deepest conscience says should never be made possible: nuclear war.

You do that through refusing to be enrolled in the military system. You can't with your own actions — voluntary training — contribute to upholding the myth that modern war is permissible under the name of defence, at the same time as your lifetime experience has taught you that the only way to save life during a situation no one can cope with, is to fight war itself."[4]

Barbro Alving's refusal was grounded in the pacifist belief she had held for decades. *Irene Andersson,* a Swedish historian who has written about *Barbro Alving* and the Swedish peace movement before World War II explains: *"The reason why Barbro Alving continued her struggle against civil defence in the 1950s, she thought herself, was the identity as a pacifist and objector she had developed two decades earlier."* [5]

In 1935 *Barbro Alving* became part of an informal network of women in Sweden who were radical pacifists and who organised the *"Women's Unarmed Uprising Against War"* in 1935. At the time she was 26 years old, and strongly admired *Elin Wägner,* another journalist and writer who played a central role in many peace organisations and initiatives in Sweden in the 1920s and 1930s, including the formation of the unarmed uprising. Wägner was a radical pacifist, inspired by Gandhi to make pacifism an active force through nonviolent resistance to war. More than 20,000 Swedish women were involved in the action one way or another. On 3 August 1935, the uprising was declared on the front page of the weekly magazine *Tidevarvet,* the text written by *Elin Wägner* [6].

This radical statement urged women all over Sweden not to take part in *the machinery of war* by accepting the logic of civil defence. Women were asked to take a personal stand against gas masks, air raid shelters and other so-called means of "protection". Since it would be impossible to protect everyone in the case of a gas attack, the women should refuse to be saved at the cost of someone else. The statement reflected the current state of affairs where men were in control of powerful positions, by arguing that women's refusal to participate in *air raid shelter and gas mask discipline* would make some men come to their senses and work for new forms of coexistence between people, when they realised that it was impossible to defend everyone against the new kind of weapons that had been developed.

Although most of the women who organised the uprising were affiliated to different organisations, they agreed that they signed it as individuals, and not as representatives of their organisations. This way they signalised that refusal was an individual responsibility, at not something connected to membership in political parties and organisations. The women who received the magazine were encouraged to nominate women to be elected for a representative assembly, a one-day women's parliament. The action turned out much bigger than the organisers had expected. More than 700 nominations came in, and around 80 women were elected to the assembly. They met in Stockholm on 1st September 1935, only one month after the publication of the initial statement. The meeting had four keynote speakers and was followed by discussions.

In her speech to the assembly, *Elin Wägner* enlarged on the topics from the statement. Among other things she said: *"Every housewife who neglects to empty her room in the attic, to paint its woodwork with a proper fireproof substance, to sprinkle a thick layer of sand on its floor, to seal up her larder against gas and secure an ice box to protect the family's food from poisoning, she is already an objector, whether she knows it or not."*[7]

At the end of the day, the assembly adopted a resolution and elected a delegation to travel to Geneva to present the statement to the League of Nations and to an international meeting of the *Women's International League of Peace and Freedom.*

The uprising was a reaction to the militarisation of everyday life, and the fact that, with new weapons like chemical gas, it was no longer possible to distinguish between the front line and civilians. It is also possible to see in the uprisings, connections to the Greek play Lysistrata, written by Aristophanes more than 2000 years ago. The play was translated into Swedish in 1932, and performed in Stockholm in 1934 [8]. In the play, the women refuse to have sex with their husbands until they end the Peloponesian war.

In the years that followed, both *Babro Alving* and *Elin Wägner* continued their struggle against war preparations and the way civilians were being sucked in by the war machinery. However, with the increasing danger of war they found it ever more difficult to find support among other women. In 1938 a huge air raid preparation exercise was planned in the capital, Stockholm. *Barbro Alving* and *Elin Wägner* planned an action together with a few other women. Their plan was to quietly walk away in a demonstration to another part of the city and read a statement against the war preparation. However, because of lack of advance support the action never took place.

What they did manage to do was to combine the protest against war preparations with the emerging question about how refugees were treated in Sweden. A proclamation called *"An act which liberates"*, signed by 50 people, appeared in the newspaper the day after the air raid exercise. In the text they said that the civil defence system that Sweden had decided to build did not create any security, and did not result in less fear. Insecurity and fear was a direct consequence of the system of war. To help protect refugees, on the other hand, was a moral obligation and would strengthen democracy and faith in humanity. They therefore called for a change in Sweden's refugee policy [9].

The following extract from the declaration of the *Women's Unarmed Uprising Against War* 1935 gives an insight to the contribution made by its supporters to the peace movement in Sweden.

Thanks to Irene Andersson for help with putting this article together.
Translation from original Swedish quotes to English by Majken Jul Sørensen.

Footnotes

[1] Andersson, Irene "En civilförsvarsvägran med rötter i 1930-talet" [A civil defence objector with roots in the 1930s] in "När Alving blev Bang" [When Alving became Bang] edited by Marcos Cantera Carlomagno, Historiska media, 2001 p. 33.
[2] Alving, Barbro (Bang), "Civilförsvaret" in "Hertha" 42(1955):3 p. 5.
[3] Alving, Barbro (Bang), "Civilförsvaret" in "Hertha" 42(1955):3 p. 5-6.
[4] Alving, Barbro (Bang), "Civilförsvaret" in "Hertha" 42(1955):3 p. 6.
[5] Andersson, Irene "En civilförsvarsvägran med rötter i 1930-talet" [A civil defence objector with roots in the 1930s] in "När Alving blev Bang" [When Alving became Bang] edited by Marcos Cantera Carlomagno, Historiska media, 2001 p. 42.
[6] Andersson, Irene "En civilförsvarsvägran med rötter i 1930-talet" [A civil defence objector with roots in the 1930s] in "När Alving blev Bang" [When Alving became Bang] edited by Marcos Cantera Carlomagno, Historiska media, 2001 p. 37.
[7] Wägner, Elin "Vad tänker du, mänsklighet" [What are you thinking, humanity], selection by Helena Forsås-Scott, Norstedts 1999.
[8] Andersson, Irene "Kvinnor mot krig – Aktioner och nätverk för fred 1914-1940" [Women against war – actions and networks for peace 1914-1940], Historiska institutionen vid Lunds universitet, 2001, p. 159.
[9] Andersson, Irene "Kvinnor mot krig – Aktioner och nätverk för fred 1914-1940" [Women against war – actions and networks for peace 1914-1940], Historiska institutionen vid Lunds universitet, 2001, p. 270-275) and "En handling som befriar" [An act which liberates], Socialdemokraten, September 9th, 1938, p. 9.

Women's Unarmed Uprising Against War, 1935

Women, join together, demand of all men that they reflect on where they are taking humankind. The wisest and best of them can see this and are trying to change the course of development: support them, insist on helping them. But demand that they lay down their weapons, then let them see that you are willing to lay down yours! Refuse to participate in the machinery of war, refuse the air raid shelter and gas mask discipline.

Women, tell them that you do not believe in gas masks, air raid shelters, and other devices for protection. Tell them that you have seen through the absurdity in trying to protect [absolutely] everyone and that you recoil from the inhumanity in the idea of some being chosen for rescue and others being left to perish. Tell them that you do not want to sacrifice your children to the poisonous gases and fires outside the over-full shelters, but neither do you wish to be rescued at the expense of someone else, only then to step out into a ravaged world. If you do this, then by virtue of their innate instincts, men will also be forced to defend their own, to make the ultimate effort to create and piece together a respect for new forms of coexistence between people.

Extract of the Women's Unarmed Uprising Against War. Quote from Andersson, Irene, "Women's Unarmed Uprising Against War: A Swedish Peace Protest in 1935" in "Journal of Peace Research" vol 40, no 4 2003, p 404-405.

Total Resistance to Military Service

We, women committed to anti-militarism and feminism, believe that total resistance to military service is the necessary role for all women challenged by the military structure in society.

We see war and violence as male attributes used to no avail over the centuries; conflicts have not been solved nor peace established. Militarism is an expression of a male structure and male violence imposed against society to the detriment of all, and in particular women.

We cannot accept a passive role in society and recognise that women must emerge as a critical force challenging the established structure dominated by militarism; but we cannot relate emancipation to the same role adopted by men, and reject the need to imitate them. We see our stand against violence, exploitation and injustice as the basis of our feminist pacifism and anti-militarist feminist.

Women war resisters and nonviolent activists recognise the long struggle undertaken predominantly by men, supported by women, in relation to their refusal to accept compulsory military service both in times of war and peace. We regard this struggle as a positive act against militarism.

We appreciate the legal steps striven for and gained by the COs' position. In most cases this has led to establishing an alternative service approved by the State in lieu of the military commitment.

Throughout this period of development and reform there has always been the total resister, both in times of war and peace, who has refused to comply with the State's demand and rejected the alternative service granted by some nations. We respect the choice of the individual whether she or he accepts the alternative service regulations or decides voluntarily on total non-co-operation.

However, we submit that the military challenge when directed to women is different and demands a radical response – we therefore urge that women commit themselves to total resistance to military and alternative service for the following reasons:

- total resistance as a rejection of militarism is a positive political choice whether based on moral, emotional, political or religious grounds
- the acceptance of alternative service while showing a refusal to take part in direct military action does not and cannot change the authoritarian, hierarchical and oppressive society represented and upheld by militarism; moreover we see it as a governmental

concession which undermines the radical content of conscientious objection and is in any case clouded by punitive measures which we find unacceptable

- in most countries women are likely to be conscripted into non-combatant duties, albeit under direct military control, not greatly different from the alternative service available to some men today (administration, health ...). By accepting this position, women will then free the men conscripts for concentrated combat training and will have put themselves into a supportive role
- recognition of an alternative service implies the recognition of the structure and purpose of the military which are not instruments of emancipation. COs may have expressed a degree of awareness by rejecting the male traditional ideology of the military. But there is no such analogy for women, who would remain in their usual feminine role
- it is equally probable that women will be called up to work in civil defence, which is likely to appeal to them because it appears to be based on humanitarian needs which reflect their traditional role as nurturers. We reject this position with equal vigour since it is only a part of the war machine and the myth of global defence.

We therefore believe that the possibility of alternative service provided for women COs cannot be accepted and that they have no alternative other than to reject any form of conscription with the military. In this way, therefore, we consider that we cannot follow the pattern of male CO history, and that women here and now must take a stand of no compromise, whether we are as yet directly involved or not.

We therefore urge that women show their intention now not to co-operate with war, thereby making it clear to governments that their emancipation has no connection with militarism, which only serves to crush the individual initiative for which we strive.

We believe we must educate women to understand the implications involved not because we see women as such as the natural peacemakers but because we do not intend to follow policies that can only lead to the exploitation of the individual, to violence and to war.

This statement was prepared by a group of women involved in the War Resisters' International and was signed by women attending the International conference on Women and Militarism, 26 July to 1 August 1980, Laurieston Hall, Laurieston, Castle Douglas, Dumfriesshire, Scotland.

German Women Said No

Discussion about women in the military

After female officers had been admitted to the medical corps in 1975 a debate about military conscription for women had started. The proposals initiated much debate in the peace and the women's movements. The feminists were divided — on one side Alice Schwarzer, the editor of the radical, German feminist magazine Emma, fronting the debate. In 1978 she argued that the military represented a too important power to be monopolised by men. Therefore she demanded the opening of the military, including all combat positions, for women, though she herself personally would apply for CO status if she were subject to military conscription. On the other side were women in the peace movement objecting in principle to women in the military. In 1979 a group of 87 women made a public statement saying: Women into the Federal Army? — We say NO! One of them was the prominent post-war writer *Luise Rinser* (1911–2002) whose furious statement is documented below.

Resistance against inclusion of women in war preparations

According to the emergency laws all German citizens are liable to be called up for civilian services in the case of war or any other emergency, with specific provision for health personnel, based on the German Constitution (Art. 12a, 4 and 6) and the emergency provisions of 1968.

In 1968 the Ministry of Defence and Ministry of Interior financed equally a four-week course as nursing assistants for women between 18 and 55 years old. This was partly because of shortage of personnel in the military and in the hospitals. The more women work in such positions, the more men are available for military service. However, in the late 1970s people became aware that the training was mainly meant for military planning. After the training the women would sign a paper that they would be available for service in case of war or emergency. In 1982 a law was proposed for further integration of health services in military structures (Gesundheitssicherstellungsgesetz).

All these forms of civilian conscription for women were seen as part of war preparations leading finally to the militarisation of society, as anti-militarist women would say. Both the proposed law and the declaration to be signed in connection with the nursing assistance courses provoked protests. Thus this bill had to be withdrawn, but the integration of civilian institutions in military planning continued and still continues.

At the time, many women in the peace movement felt that they had to make a statement as conscientious objectors. As part of the campaign — which included marches and other public protests — women produced a petition to be signed and sent it to the Federal Office for Civilian Service (Bundesamt für Zivildienst). We present the text of the petition here. We present also Claudia Schneider's protest letter to the Office for Civil Security and the response she got.

Many of the feminists and leftists — such as Communists and Social Democrats — who protested against the proposals to conscript women for civilian war services in case of war nevertheless at the same time supported the existing military conscription of men and refused to support male total resisters.

Introduction by Ellen Elster
Thanks to Helga Weber Zucht and Gernot Lennert for help with translation and finding information.

Re: Objecting to Conscription of Women

In regard to Article No. 12A, Paragraph 4 and 6 of the Basic Law (constitution), women of the age between 18 and 55 may be conscripted for civilian services should the country be forced to defend itself.

I am declaring herewith, that I do not accept such a possible obligation and that I will not fulfil it at any time. My reasons are as follows:

Such a civilian service will in the end only support war, and the inclusion of helpers in civilian and military areas will support war preparation. These civilian services are therefore to be considered war services and as such I will refuse them.

Especially now in so-called time of peace, I have to defend myself against a possible conscription – as the danger of a war is constantly growing through the politics of armament and deterrence. Wars are being prepared during peace times.

I understand my refusal as a contribution to an active peace policy.

Besides, please be aware that I am totally against any kind of inclusion of women into military services.

Thank you in advance for a statement of confirming your receipt of my letter.

Signature

Printed in a leaflet produced by DFG-VK, the German section of War Resisters' International, in the beginning of the 1980's.

Regarding liability to national service in case of need to defend the country in case of war

In September 1979 I took part in training for nursing assistance with the Malteser Aid Service in Freiburg. At the end of the training we had to sign a form thereby committing ourselves to render service in case of war ("Ernstfall"), ie medical services in civilian as well as military contexts.

I am declaring herewith that I refuse and will be refusing military service at any time. I am not willing to support violence – and war is always violence – in any shape, not even in the first aid area. Herewith I am informing you as well that I will not follow any call for conscription, as is planned for women in the German Constitution Art. 12a, 4.

My reasons:

I abhor violence and war and will not support in any way. Human beings do not want either of them, yet there are again and again attempts to spread fear and suspicion about imagined enemies. I do not believe that violence will help changing the world. I have no enemies. Our people has no enemies. This conviction enables me to live without the protection of weapons and I am not willing to support violence. This civilian service is serving war after all, and the knowledge about the availability of helpers in the civilian and medical areas facilitates the preparation of wars. Therefore it is important to inform the Government that I am not willing to obey such a service obligation.

Letter by Claudia Schneider to the Office for Civil Security, Karlsruhe, 17th January 1979.

Dear Miss Schneider!

Your ideologically flavoured letter has been forwarded to me by the Office for Civil Security. I am shuddering to hear that you, as a trained nursing assistant, will be refusing to help citizens who might be injured or in need of help in case of a catastrophe or a plague, eg that you are refusing to help and care for women and children, unlike the common law of humanity would think it natural for any decent person. The Swiss civilian Henry Dunant, after whom the street you are living in was named, did not hesitate to help and give first aid to severely injured people in a war he abhorred. He helped transporting them, feeding them and wrote nice letters for those who were dying. It would be really bad for humankind and for humanity, if there were only Claudia Schneiders, who refuse to give aid to their brothers and sisters whose life is in danger. The Office for Civil Security as well as the State Health Office is happy to do without the cooperation of such hard-hearted persons.

Reply by Dr. Pfannkuch, State Medical Director in Office, State Health Office Karlsruhe (Staatliches Gesundheitsamt Karlsruhe), 12th March 1979.

Both letters printed in Graswurzelrevolution, probably at the beginning of the 1980s.

How stupid we women are

I am totally against the concept of "Women in the Army". The whole women's movement for emancipation is a farce, if equality means that also women should be allowed to shoot human beings. In addition, this is being dictated by men. The late Erich Fromm called this the "Necrophilia": Fascination by death and by killing. Oh my god, how stupid we women are: We willingly conform to exactly that senselessness, which we do not want any longer. Hopelessness: Woman.

Instead of getting men to stop killing, women are aiming now, to do what he should not do any longer. That's foolishness. Really. Women are becoming men. Patriarchy keeps continuing without any shame, because the male soldier-spirit continues to exist. Whether women or men are shooting makes no difference. I am nearly giving up any hope that patriarchy will ever be overcome. ....

Luise Rinser

Published in "Deutsche Volkszeitung", 15th May 1980.

French Women Say "Non à la guerre"

A framework for female objection to military service was one of the fruits of the *"Assises de l'objection"*, a three-day meeting on CO issues organised by the Le Cun du Larzac community in southern France.

The conference and its workshops examined all — or nearly all — aspects of objection, from the pressures on scientists to collaborate with the military establishment, to the militarisation of education, to the role of churches on objection, to war tax resistance. The workshop on women and militarism, which was open to both sexes, addressed a long-standing problem — the potential mobilisation of women in times of war.

A 1959 law provides for the *"requisition of female personnel may apply under the same conditions, and subject to the same penalties, as male personnel"*. As an indication of the state's intentions to militarise the whole of French society, this law has provoked considerable attention since its promulgation. At the Larzac meeting, a "statut d'objectrice" — a demand for conscientious objector status for women — was agreed and made available for women to sign.

Promulgation du Statut d'objectrice: promulgation of the status of female objection

According to the ordinance of 1959 women are mobilised for the general organisation of defence on the same basis as men.

Defence is a permanent state which foresees and allows in all circumstances and at all times the mobilisation of military and civilians, men and women, under the same authority and with the same obligations in case of threat; according to internal or external tensions, one or several sectors of the country's activities can be put directly under the direction and responsibility of the military.

As antimilitarist women in struggle for the recognition of our rights, we denounce:

- the army as a means of perpetuating the dominance of women by men, for the macho ideology, the prestige of the uniform, the cult of violence, the reproduction of the patriarchal model by authority, by hierarchy.
- the proliferation, around military bases around the world, of prostitution, rape and sexual abuse among the population the military is supposed to "protect".

Due to the 1959 ordinance, and other encouragements that they should consider careers in the military, women cannot consider themselves outside the military system.

We refuse to participate in the repression of social movements.

We have an important role to play in the sectors subject to military requisition – that is, health, education, communication, transport, and public service, in order to block the process of militarisation and refuse to collaborate with it.

For all these reasons, we declare ourselves to be conscientious objectors (objectrices de conscience) to any such requisition, refusing to subject ourselves to the service of defence.

Peace News, August 1991. Abridged from report in the Belgian MIR-IRG magazine L'Objecteur, July 1991.

Women Conscientious Objectors in Belgium

By Rebecca Gumbrell McCormick

At the end of 1985 the *Mouvement International de la Réconciliation — International des Resistants à la Guerre* (MIR-IRG), one of the Belgian affiliates of the WRI, together with the conscientious objectors' group *Confederation du Service Civil de la Jeunesse* (CSCJ), launched an appeal for Belgian women to declare themselves COs. Since then, several women have sent requests for conscientious objector status to the Minister of the Interior, who has rejected them all as "non-recevable". What are the reasons for this seemingly fruitless action?

Background

The Belgian demand for the extension of conscientious objection to women, and others not covered under current legislation, is based on the desire to extend the protection of CO status to all those who share the philosophical objection to militarism of COs. At present, men who have been exempted from military service for another reason, such as having done development work in the Third World, foreigners resident in Belgium, and women, are not subject to conscription, and cannot register as COs. The CO's statutory right not to bear arms, serve the military, or work in the defence industry, is not now granted to others with the same moral conviction.

At the same time, Belgian citizens now exempt from conscription are specifically included in a 1984 law on "*civil protection*" which permits the Ministry of the Interior to assign citizens to "*tasks of general interest*" in the event of national emergency. Without the protection of CO status, there may be no way for these citizens to refuse tasks with a military application or organisation. This law has been challenged on a number of grounds, and has never been put into practice.

More important at present is the lack of legal defence for those not granted CO status against other forms of militarisation, particularly in employment. A former conscientious objector may not bear arms or be employed in an arms industry or in any other work with a military application, until he reaches the age of 45. During that time, he is therefore protected against any demand from the unemployment service that he accept a job, for which he is otherwise qualified, in the defence industry. No one else has this automatic protection. For all those who have come to reflect on the moral dilemma of work in industries that produce nuclear weapons or supply arms to dictatorial regimes too late to demand CO status, it is an injustice. For women, who cannot register as COs, it is also a clear case of sex discrimination.

46

The Campaign

For these and other reasons, the Belgian peace movement and CO groups have decided to demand the extension of conscientious objection to women and others not covered by the present law. In 1983 the Socialist Senator Lydia De Pauw-Deveen proposed a series of reforms of the CO statutes, including its extension to women. Her reforms were not voted into law, but won the support of many women legislators not associated with the Left or the Socialist Party.

COs and peace groups have now decided to pursue their campaign by calling on women to file for CO status. Those who have written to the Ministry of the Interior so far have stressed their opposition to defence work and nuclear weapons, and their support of the same moral and philosophical principles as COs.

The following letter was written by a woman named Josiane:

Since May 1 1985 I have been unemployed. I do not now have the right to refuse employment in the arms industry or in any industry requiring the bearing of arms without losing my unemployment benefits. As a social worker by profession, I have observed the decline in the national budget for jobs in the social sector, despite its contribution to development and to a better way of life. Our national defence policy promotes the arms race ... arms which can destroy our planet dozens of times.

I do not feel protected by the perpetual nuclear threat, especially since last March, we have had nuclear missiles in our territory. I am now seven months pregnant, and it is my duty as a woman to protect life and to act in consequence. I think that it is necessary for Belgium to envisage a system of effective defence to provide for the genuine security of persons, their fulfilment and democratic freedom.

The holocaust threatened by our current system must be prevented. The only sensible and life-affirming course is to stop this suicidal arms race, find an intelligent manner to recycle our missiles and remove their destructive capacity, and spend our money instead on a serious defence; one which promotes the welfare and potential of adults and children at all levels, gives suitable work to young people, and looks for ways to convert our arms industries.

Reflections

It is too soon to tell how many more women will ask for CO status. If the campaign succeeds, women may still not be legally accepted as COs, but they will have come to play a more active part in the male-dominated Belgian peace movement, thereby greatly increasing its effectiveness. Furthermore, the demand for CO status for women would fit into the broader campaign for conscientious objection to defence work, conversion of the arms industry and the development of a new popular defence strategy. This campaign, in Belgium and in many other countries, has done much to broaden the scope of the peace movement and connect it with other forces working for social change.

There are however a number of pitfalls in this campaign. Most importantly, it could be seen as indirect support of the principle of conscription. CO status for women would imply the acceptance of alternative civilian service, because rights imply obligations. Alternative service is rarely the genuine peace service its advocates intended, and in fact often creates low-cost competition with regularly-employed workers in the social sector — many of them women. Not only that; their demand for CO status might be used as an argument for the actual conscription of women into military service. In the end, the campaign would have created new obligations for women while leaving in place one already in force for men.

This eventuality would truly be a step backwards. However, without denying the force of this reservation, is it not also true that to do nothing in the face of the growing militarisation of society would be to take two steps backward? In Belgium, legal protection is needed against the law forcing tasks of a potentially military character on women, and others not now subject to conscription; in many countries, such protection is needed for all those forced to undertake tasks with a military application in the course of their work. CO status would help both groups.

Furthermore, alternative civilian service, despite is shortcomings, might give women an opportunity to play a more active role in the political and social sectors where most COs are affected.

As an argument, the demand for conscientious objection for women is a far better basis for a positive campaign for peace and equality than the popular view, the logic of which is not immediately apparent, that women as mothers, nurturers and so on are especially great lovers of peace (as in the letter above). Instead of seeking to maintain women in a special category, the demand for the broadening of the concept of conscientious objection promotes equal rights for women and greater rights for everybody, and provides at least one of the moral and legal weapons needed to fight back against militarism in society.

Despite the above reservations, the Belgian campaign merits our further reflection and argument. It could contribute to the greater involvement of women in the struggle for peace in many countries, and lead to broader and more effective campaigns.

Printed originally in WRI Women No 1, Jan/Feb 1987, the newsletter of the Women's Working group of War Resisters' International. At the time of writing, the author was vice-Chair of the European Bureau for Conscientious Objection, but she says in a footnote that the views expressed in the article are her own.

"Coffee Serving Resistance"? An Introduction to Women's Conscientious Objection in Israel

Israel is one of two countries currently with conscription of women. Through the stories and declarations we are presenting here, we see a development from objection for religious reasons to reasons of conscience in 1954, and later for more political reasons in 1970 and up till to-day. The Six-Day war in 1967 seems to be a turning point. The last declaration we are presenting is from April 2009, after the bombing of Gaza.

Sergeiy Sandler [1] writes [2] that Israeli society is highly militarised. Children in kindergartens often stage a military parade at their end of the year party. A few years later, they are likely to study some of their regular curriculum subjects with teachers who are conscripts in military uniform. The head teacher of the high school where they study later in life might well be a medium-ranked military officer, who recently retired from career service. Conscription is a central instrument of political power and a major issue on the political agenda. Social inequalities are reproduced, reinforced and often created by the conscription policy of the army. Thus, members of the Palestinian minority among Israeli citizens are not called up to military service, and this fact is then used as an excuse for official and unofficial discrimination against them in all spheres of life. For instance, when an employer is looking for a worker *"with military service completed"*, it would be a code for *"Arabs not wanted"*. Jewish women are drafted, but they are required to serve a shorter term of military service (2 years, as opposed to 3 years for men) and are given functions within the military that are deemed unimportant. This is reflected in women's social status and in their marginalisation in the public sphere (for instance, women make up less than 10% of the Israeli parliament). Opinions of generals on public matters are considered authoritative.

There is an active and large movement of women draft resisters in Israel, the only one of its kind in the world. Israeli conscription legislation is also anomalous in that a conscientious objector status is recognised for women only. This fact sets women objectors as a distinct group apart from their male counterparts. *Shani Werner* raised the issue of what it meant to be a conscientious objector woman in a letter in 2002 [3], in relation to the first Seniors' (*Shministim*) Open Letter [4] in 2001 which was written by young women and men draft resisters. The following is an extract from Shani's letter:

> "It didn't occur to us then to ask ourselves whether both kinds of resistance (women's and men's) belonged together. We were so convinced that women's draft resistance is identical in importance to men's, that we weren't even aware of the significance we had given the letter in placing women's and men's resistance on the same plane. Personally, I only came

to internalise this significance when faced with people's responses – "What's that supposed to mean?" or – "Way to go!" I felt we had done something special and important.

It's been a long time now, over a year and a half. Gradually, I got frustrated. I started feeling how inside our protective "hothouse", the Seniors' in particular, and that of the Israeli Left in general, we had made a mirror-image of just what we set out to oppose. We had militarised draft resistance! (...)

Of course, the resistance of the boys-men is very important. And we, the girls-women resisters outside of prison, take care to support and encourage the resisters doing time inside. But I think the pattern of behavior initially arising from the fact that "the men are in prison, and the women get exempted from service" has set and hardened into certain patterns of thought. (...)

My refusal to enlist in the army, which I used to see as a political-public act, has now become private. ("The personal is the political" – the mantra runs through my head. But the personal only becomes political when it is allowed a voice!) As public discourse is unaware of it, as the discourse of the Left ignores it, the draft resistance of girls-women remains personal, not to say silenced. It's precisely as easy for us to ignore women's draft resistance as it is for the IDF to ignore women's military service. If women's service in the army is seen, in any case, as relatively easily, our resistance is treated like "coffee serving resistance," which even the army accepts (and if the army doesn't need us, unlike the imprisoned boys, then can our resistance have any significance?)."

In the following we bring, briefly, a few stories of women refusing the military, the first ones as early as 1954. In the main contributions, *Tali Lerner* writes about the complexity of women's roles in Israeli society as well as how they are mirrored in the military, and the role of being a woman conscientious objector. This article is followed by *Idan Halili*'s contribution. She is telling her own story of becoming a feminist and then the consequences of turning out to be a conscientious objector. Lastly, you will find the first Seniors' letter from 2001 (Shministim) which is referred to several times in the following texts.

Introduction by Ellen Elster

References

[1] Sergeiy Sandler is an activist in New Profile and a Council and Executive member of WRI.
[2] The information is from an article Sergeiy Sandler wrote in Broken Rifle No 58, May 2003.
[3] Shani Werner: Letter to the Israeli refuser movement, 31 December 2002.
[4] Printed in this section.

Chava Bloch

WAR RESISTERS

ISRAEL

Chava Bloch, the only non-religious female resister, has been asked several times to appear before a commission which is to enquire into her reasons for refusal to be inducted, but each time the hearing has been postponed.

The War Resister No 64. Spring 1954.

Hagar and Ruth Lisser — Schoolgirl Conscientious Objectors

SCHOOLGIRL CONSCIENTIOUS OBJECTORS

J. W. Abileah writes from Israel that Hagar and Ruth, daughters of W.R.I. members Paul and Sabina Lisser, recently refused to undertake compulsory youth training (Gadna) at their school. Hagar, who is sixteen, was warned that persistent refusal might prevent her from taking the final examinations. Both girls were finally excused, however, without punishment.

Gadna involves two hours per week, plus six days a year, plus ten days concentrated training in camp. Our W.R.I. Section in Israel has protested against this, pointing out that militarisation is plainly contrary to Israel's mission, and asking "shall we really betray the vision of our prophets while their praise is on our lips?"

The War Resister No 65. Summer 1954.

Tovah

Tovah was born in 1953 in the town Afulah, which is just south of Nazareth in the Jesreel Valley. ... Tovah is one of three or four women in Israel today [1970] who was exempted from military service for reasons of conscience. The law states that women may be exempted from service for reasons of conscience and religion. Many women have been exempted in religious grounds but only three or four have insisted to be released on grounds of conscience. It was during her third year of high school that she decided to refuse to serve in the army. *"I did not have any connections to any organizations. I had only my ideas. ... Then when I was seventeen, during vacation, I went to the army office in Haifa and announced there my refusal to go to the army. I said I did not want to go to the army because I am against violence. ...*

... A woman from the committee [in charge of exemption of women from active service] asked if I belonged to any pacifist groups. I said no. She said 'Then, you are not a pacifist.' One person asked if I knew about World War II, 'Six million were killed and you do not want to go to the army.' A woman from the committee, who was fair, said to the other officer that 'There is no connection between the six million and her ideas.' After this committee, I went before a second committee. They said 'We think you can be very useful for the army.' So I said, 'Yes, I can spread pacifism in the army. I will be very useful.' 'If we do not release you from the army, what are you going to do?' I said 'I am not going to tell you my tactics. For example, I will not be afraid to go to jail because I strongly believe that if I am sent to jail it is not because I am a criminal, but because I do not want to be a criminal.' After this meeting I was released from the army." ...

Tovah believes that people do not understand the problem of Israel because they have not been able to break away from the illusion that the government is good. Now, those that do break with this illusion are treated as enemies of the government. ... Tovah asserts that once many people begin to argue with themselves and question the government, the military and the government will begin to break.

"The 1967 War was important because in its aftermath the attitudes of the people who refused to serve in the army and the attitudes of the government changed. Before the war, the people who refused to serve did so out of principle. ... The basic pacifist idea was refusal to hold a

gun and to serve in the military, or any army. But now it is not only against guns; Now it is much more concrete. People now oppose what the army is doing — its policies in the occupied territories against citizens; the oppression of citizens, the terrorizing of people. ... "

The situation in Israel is more acute now than ever before. Tovah states that the Arabs are in a worse position now than they have been in the past. Because she sees Zionism, a force that discriminates against non-Jews, as the cause of this development, Tovah considers herself anti-Zionist. She maintains that a cosmopolitan or internationalist worldview is the way towards peace. *"That is why I am cosmopolitan. Hatred is war. Hatred is blood. Hatred is killing people. It is good that more people are refusing to serve and that people are beginning to understand the nature of the Israeli government."*

Tovah's story is derived from chapter 10, page 103-107, in Dissent & Ideology in Israel. Resistance to the Draft 1948-1973, edited by Martin Blatt, Uri Davis, Paul Kleinbaum. Published by Ithaca Press London 1975 for Housmans Bookshop, WRI, MERAG (The Middle East Research & Action Group and The Lansbury House Trust Fund).

Conscientious objector Neta Mishli sentenced to 20 days imprisonment

Neta Mishli, 18, from Tel-Aviv, a signatory of the 2008 high school seniors refusal letter, began serving her first prison term on 23 April 2009. Neta Mishli arrived at the military Induction Base on 22 April and refused to enlist. For this she was first sentenced to seven days of confinement to base (she was told there was no room in the military prison for women). However, the following day she was again tried and sentenced, this time to 20 days in military prison. She was told that the Military Attorney's Office has authorized trying her again for the very same act.

Neta Mishli has prepared the following declaration upon entering prison:

"I am not willing to be part of an organisation committing war crimes, taking the lives of thousands of innocent civilians, an organization that, in the name of humanism and democracy, forces me and my peers to sacrifice a period of our lives, and our lives themselves, for false calm, for no calm shall come to pass until Israel decides to give up the policy of war and turn towards peace. Therefore, as a small step towards stopping the cycle of bloodshed, I hereby refuse to enlist in the military."

Neta Mishli is due to be released from prison on 10 May, but is likely to be imprisoned again soon afterwards.

This text was first published as a CO-alert, War Resisters' International, London, 24 April 2009. From: concodoc@wri-irg.org

On Women's Refusal in Israel

By Tali Lerner, New Profile

C itizenship in Israel is judged in terms of the relations between a certain group and the military. Ultra-orthodox Jewish or Arab citizens are perceived as second-rate citizens. This is legitimised because they are exempted from compulsory military service. By contrast, other social groups, for instance, the Bedouins and the Druze, as well as members of the gay-lesbian community, by contrast, rest their claim for equal citizenship on their equal share in shouldering the burden of the country's security. Women's relations with the state, and with the army in particular, are even more complex. Women's right to vote and their duty to enlist were affirmed with the establishment of the state — indeed, Israel is one of the few countries in the world that has compulsory military service for women. As a result, the state accepts women's citizenship in terms of their taking equal part in military service, yet at the same time also excludes them because women cannot become truly equal members of the military organisation and take equal part in military duties. This creates serious complexities for the local feminist and antimilitarist movements. Women's refusal to enlist is therefore a very complicated phenomenon, reflecting some basic feminist dilemmas.

The Discourse on Citizenship in Israel

From its very inception — and even before it — military service (or service in the paramilitary groups that preceded the Israeli army) was always a central social institution. A movement for national renewal, Zionism, and later Israel, purported to create a new Jewish individual who would come to replace the old stereotype of an effeminate, physically and morally weak person. Military organisations played a crucial role in the shaping of the ideal Zionist individual. This intense equation between the citizen and the soldier became more and more entrenched as the state and its institutions evolved. Reference to the individual citizen's military service is universal: it filters through the most basic levels of talk about civil society; it is in the workplace, and plays a role in getting a driving licence or in any other formal exchanges with the authorities.

When we zoom into specific social groups, the situation is even more problematic. The interrelations between so-called *"minority groups"* and mainstream society are very often defined in terms of their position vis a vis the army. There is considerable pressure to make the connection between citizenship and army service direct and unambiguous, which would in effect mean depriving entire social groups who don't serve of their right to citizenship. This is how Arab or ultra-orthodox Jewish citizens of Israel — who are legally exempted from compulsory enlistment — become second-class citizens. It is by pointing at this fact that the state explains its discriminatory practices toward them. Other groups, for instance the Arabic Bedouin or the Druze, appeal to the fact that they enlist in support of their demand for equal citizenship. As Arabs, they are indeed better socially accepted than their non-serving counterparts. Similarly, there are relatively many gay men who quote how they have made their *"contribution to shouldering the burden of national security"* when trying to justify their right to equal citizenship and when demanding recognition as a legitimate group in Israeli society. Israeli society, therefore, was founded, and continues to be based, on military service as an entry ticket for citizenship and adult participation in Israeli society.

On Women, Military Service, and Citizenship in Zionist Society — A Historical Perspective

It is, to begin with, important to have some idea about the context of the encounter between the Israeli feminist movement and the army, as well as society at large. Women received the right to vote in the various institutions of the Zionist movement even before the foundation of the state. Women's participation in society was defined according to the socialist model that put the individual's contribution to the collective as its central value. Women were seen to constitute, in their own way, an equal part of that contribution. The notion of the female pioneer was integral to the Zionist enterprise. At the same time, as a result of women's own activism, they were also included in the Zionist community's first combatant bodies that preceded the Israeli army — the paramilitary *Palmakh* and the *Haganah*. With the establishment of the state and the Israeli army their compulsory service was self-evident.

Nevertheless, it was decided as early as the Independence War — especially now that the army had become a true *"people's army"*, including not only, as it had before, the more liberal pioneers — to create the women's forces, which would include the various tasks that were suitable for women, and to stop allowing women to serve in combatant roles. At the same time the exemption from compulsory military service for religious women was instituted, so that these women would not be forced, against their religious principle, into mixed work conditions with men. A considerable percentage of women in Israel were exempted from military service through this channel.

From a contemporary, critical perspective, women in the early period of the Zionist movement can already be seen to be excluded from significant functions, and we can identify a conservative gender ideal of the woman as mother and educator who makes it possible for her husband to go out, build the land and participate in the country's wars. Nevertheless, for many years, the society was dominated by a relatively egalitarian ethos according to which women, though kept out of certain important social roles, were still seen as having a significant and, as it were, equal position in Israeli society.

The Feminist Revolution Comes to the Israeli Army

The feminist movement in Israel, for many years, indeed until the 1990s, showed little interest in the subject of military service, and the fact that women are obliged to serve — though not so many of them, and for a shorter time, and performing a limited number of functions.

In 1995, a young woman, *Alice Miller*, appealed to the Supreme Court against the Israeli army and air force and demanded to be allowed to apply for pilot training — a prestigious military training closed to women until then. This legal action rocked gender-relations in the context of Israel's military system. Men's unwillingness to open these highly regarded places to women, because they considered them exclusively theirs, was laid bare, and the local feminist movement realised it had a new point on its agenda.

The opportunity for the feminist movement was ideal. Making the army one's reference point in formulating and demanding citizenship and equality can be a formidable tool for action. Women would be able to enter places in the military that had been inaccessible to them hitherto, then to advance to more highly regarded and influential positions in civic society. If women would be truly equal partners in shouldering the burden of security, they would be seen as "more" equal to men — and this in turn would lead to reducing the oppression of women because they were seen as weak, both physically and politically.

And like many other movements struggling for political and social rights, the Israeli feminist movement opted to embrace the army, to encourage enlistment, support access to various army functions for women, and, on the whole, struggle for women's rights within the context of military service.

Fifteen years later, we now have combatant women and women fighter pilots, and there are more female senior officers than ever. The percentage of women in secretarial roles has dropped, while the percentage of women who actually enlist has significantly risen.

So is everything all right, then? Can we really say that the road to women's equality is via high enlistment figures, equal national duty to serve, and women's volunteering to army careers?

There are other voices within the feminist movement. Some of these argue that the military system inherently includes sexual harassment as normative practice — something that obviously does not do anything to advance women; others claim that whatever change happened in the army, it has not been true change and should not be accepted as such. The main source of criticism originates in the radical elements of the Israeli feminist movement, which combines its feminist struggle with a struggle against the Occupation and against violence.

A Radical Critique of the Relations between the Army and the Feminist Movement

A more radical feminist approach than the one described above has been taking shape in the last decade. There are groups that have jointly articulated a different way of thinking about the interrelations between the military and the oppression of women as a result of a more inclusive understanding of forms of oppression, and of feminist and antimilitarist activism.

These groups — with *New Profile* taking a central place among them — consider the army, which by definition regards violence and armed combat as a way of solving problems, as also perpetuating a notion of the "warrior" as the ideal, normative man. It is around this figure that an entire social environment emerges, as part of a social process whereby people are persuaded to identify with the role of the fighter. The consecration of combat brings along a consecration of conventional masculinity and physical force. Within the hierarchy of such a military system, women will always feature as the weaker ones physically and they will be allotted inferior positions. This military structure will then impose its values via a stereotypical conception of men, which society conveys through its general socialisation processes.

When a social system is constructed on the basis of control (whether this is within the confines of a military hierarchy or enacted towards an occupied population), power and control will characterise interrelations in that society These in turn further entrench patriarchal values in the society that is already dominated by military values — in the family, in the workplace, and in politics. The very same people which the army puts in positions of power, based on a hierarchy of physical prowess, will also tend to accede to such power positions in civil society — and thus they import an entire set of military values which sanctions combat, violence, gender-based hierarchy, and power-based interpersonal relations.

These observations have been confirmed by recent research. Thus Dr *Orna Sasson-Levi* writes in her book *Identities in Uniform* [1] — based on thorough research she conducted in co-operation with the Israeli army — that women in military combat functions will adopt an alternative masculine identity rather than an alternative feminine identity, which in effect means that they are in denial of their feminine identity. Sasson-Levi identifies a similar pattern among those Israeli men who for some reason are not in harmony with the identity of the *"male fighter"*. Another study, conducted at Ben Gurion University, explains the failed integration of women into the air force as mainly due to their not having the *"mentality"* that suits pilots.

Disagreement among Feminists about the Occupation, Army, and Violence

We may learn a lot from our behaviour, both as individuals and as members of a group, in situations when there is a clash between two components of our identity. A split has occurred within Israel's feminist movement over our stance toward the Occupation, the army and violence. This shows, in my opinion, that the part of our identity that consists in our attitude towards violence is more important to our sense of self-identity than that associated with the feminist struggle. On either side of the conflicting attitudes toward the Occupation, we see women who tend to co-operate with those who, although opposing the feminist struggle, identify with their attitudes towards use of violence and the army.

It is against the background of this complex state of affairs that women's refusal in Israel calls into question a variety of myths — prevalent in the feminist movement on one hand, and in the resistance against the Occupation and the army on the other.

Women's Refusal in Israel — Facing the Army and Facing the Refusal Movement

For many years, women's refusal in Israel overlapped with the debate over issues concerning women's enlistment. The legal clause concerning exemption of religious women from compulsory military service was formulated in a way that could include exemption on any conscientious grounds — whether religious or otherwise — and it was relatively easy for young women to procure such an exemption. Hence, until 2002, there are only few recorded cases of women who were sentenced for refusal — or were, alternatively, forced to enlist against their will. Women refusers were part of activist groups against military enlistment, but they usually did not act in direct confrontation with the army like the men who refused publicly and were imprisoned or dragged into a legal struggle. The women therefore remained outside the public debate on the issue. All this changed with the 2001 *Seniors' Letter* (see the letter printed in full elsewhere in this chapter) both as regards the army's attitude to women, and as regards the women's stance vis-a-vis the refusal movement and their own role in it.

Protest against the place of women in the refusal movement came from the women themselves. The large group of female activists who were involved in this process felt that the power relations within the refusal community were replicating the oppressive gendered patterns of power distribution in society. Women who were active in this period say: *"While women in mainstream society stand on the sidelines and wave at their heroic male fighters, we stood at the prison gates, waving at our heroes as they went into jail. We stayed stuck in the role of eternal supporters and caregivers. Our own refusal took second place to our support of their refusal."* Young women activists from the *Seniors' Letter*, in collaboration with *New Profile*, started collecting women's testimonies about their refusal; they organised a study day dedicated to women's refusal, and generally began to speak out about women's refusal. The women's rejection of their role caused much friction in the refusal movement. Unfortunately change, when it came, did not happen as a result of the success of feminist values, but simply as a result of a change of army policy regarding refusal.

At the very same time that scores of refusers were being jailed for periods stretching between two months and two years, the army was conducting a lengthy legal procedure against five male refusers at the military court. *Haggai Matar*, one of these five jailed refusers, had submitted a letter explaining his conscientious objection against enlistment in the Israeli army which was almost identical to a letter written by *Hadas Goldman*, who had obtained an exemption on grounds of conscience. Haggai and his fellow refusers appealed against the discrimination between men and women in cases of exemption on grounds of conscientious objection. The military authorities reacted by tightening the criteria for what qualified as female conscientious objection and from this point on they started putting women who refused to serve and referred to the Occupation into jail. One of the first young women who was jailed as a result was *Laura Milo*, who appealed to the Supreme Court against the Minister of Defence. Subsequently an outrageous court ruling stated that an exemption on grounds of conscience should only be given for religious reasons. In practice, what this meant was that the treatment of women, in the case of conscientious objection, was made equal to that of men. Another Supreme Court ruling forced the army to regulate its routines around the so-called conscience committee and make them release men and women only for reasons of total pacifism, rejecting any other form of conscientious objection (like, for instance, refusal due to the Occupation, or indeed any articulation of pacifism that did not strike the committee as absolute). These developments brought significant change to the map of declared refusal in Israel, requiring women to face a rigid conscience committee. While many still choose to appear before the conscience committee and thus avoid imprisonment, we witness scores of female and male refusers who — in the main — make it their choice to tie their imprisonment to the anti-Occupation campaign.

Idan Halili — Feminist Refuser

Having been declined a hearing at the army's conscience committee, *Idan Halili* presented herself at the national induction centre and declared her refusal to serve in the Israeli army in October 2005. Idan wrote a four-page letter, detailing the feminist conscientious reasons why she refused to enlist. Among her arguments were, that a feminist approach clashes with violent ways of solving problems; that the military system actually harms women, within the army and in society at large, and that by her feminist thinking, the notion of equality achieved by means of military service is not a serious and valid approach to questions of equality. After spending two weeks in jail, Idan was allowed — after all — to appear before the army's conscience committee. The committee chose not to exempt her on grounds of conscience, since Idan did not prove she was a pacifist, but let her go due to incompatibility. Idan's refusal gained sympathetic responses from the feminist movement in Israel, including both its radical and less radical parts, who all identified with her criticism of the army's role in the oppression of women. Once she was released from jail, Idan voiced her disapproval of the tendency to turn those who go to jail into heroes as a way of adding legitimacy to their political statement.

Female Refusers in Jail

Six women were jailed for refusal to enlist in the course of the summer of 2008 — two more are on their way at the time of writing this. The *Seniors' Letter* of 2008 includes mostly women. Unlike so far, the army now is very reluctant to release women refusers once they have been jailed, or to exempt them from military service. These women therefore go in and out of jail for long periods of time. Because this most recent group of high school seniors includes so many young women, their letter attracted more than the usual amount of media attention. Society's attitude towards young women with a vocal social agenda is kinder than towards young men, who are expected to take their responsibility for the security of Israel more seriously.

As things stand currently, the nonviolent feminist movement's major mission is to look for non-heroic forms of refusal, forms that do not rely on the figure of the — either male or female — hero and on an ethic of self-sacrifice. Our movement must be able to offer an alternative to the conventional public discourse which so strongly builds on a notion of heroism, as well as to our own tendency to include the ethics of self-sacrifice in our political struggle.

Thanks to Mirjam Hadar for translation from Hebrew to English

Footnote

[1] Orna Sasson-Levy, 2006. Identities in Uniform: Masculinities and femininities in the Israeli Military, Jerusalem: Eshkolot series, Magnes Press, and Tel Aviv: Migdarim Series, Hakibutz Hameucahd Press (in Hebrew).

To Prime Minister Ariel Sharon

We the undersigned, youths who grew up and were brought up in Israel, are about to be called to serve the IDF. We protest before you against the aggressive and racist policy pursued by the Israeli government and its army, and to inform you that we do not intend to take part in the execution of this policy.

We strongly resist Israel's pounding of human rights. Land expropriation, arrests, executions without a trial, house demolition, closure, torture, and the prevention of health care are only some of the crimes the state of Israel carries out, in blunt violation of international conventions it has ratified. These actions are not only illegitimate; they do not even achieve their stated goal — increasing the citizens' personal safety. Such safety will be achieved only through a just peace agreement between the Israeli government and the Palestinian people.

Therefore we will obey our conscience and refuse to take part in acts of oppression against the Palestinian people, acts that should properly be called terrorist actions. We call upon persons our age, conscripts, soldiers in the standing army, and reserve service soldiers to do the same.

This letter, written by Israeli Shministim (12th graders), was sent to Israeli PM Ariel Sharon on 3 Sep 2001. Here, we only print the letter, and not the list of signatories.

An Israeli Woman's Story – A Bold Act of Refusal

By Idan Halili, New Profile

The story of how I got discharged from army service ended in 2005, when I was 19 years old. In this chapter I try to describe the story of my refusal, the process I went through, and its implications.

It was my belief then, and it still is today, that army service would force me to take part in an organisation whose principles clash with the feminist values in which I believe, and which are reflected in the commitment to human dignity, equality, consideration for the specific needs of various groups and individuals within the population, and a rejection of oppression.

I have not always defined myself as a feminist. Even though I witnessed various forms of injury to women from an early age, and always responded with shock and anger, it took me a long time to understand the profound connection between these events. Even though I came across many scores of instances of women's oppression over the years, it took serious immersion in feminist theories and active work against these injustices to really understand how these various aspects of women's oppression are interconnected.

In the eleventh grade I joined the "Hotline for Migrant Workers" where I learned a lot about trafficking in women and prostitution. I also started giving talks about these issues. This intensive activity around the trafficking in women and prostitution, amongst the most extreme outcomes of women's oppression in society, made me think a great deal about feminism and to take more of an interest in it. This is when I started to see the way that all these types of exploitation of women are tied together. I saw that women's representations in advertising, sexual harassment and trafficking all are expressions of the basic inequality of women in our society.

I had been educated to regard the army as a beneficent organisation, and I believed that the best and most obvious way to be of use to society and my country was through serving in the army. I intended to enlist and so I started the selection process to get drafted for military intelligence, with strong motivation. I thought that women's participation in the army, just like men's, was the feminist solution and would bring equality.

I decided to postpone my enlistment in order to do one year's community service at a therapeutic residential school. While working there, my feminist awareness of women's social hardships led me to run a girls' group. This provided a very powerful encounter with how women and girls internalise social messages that are destructive to them. I became more active, took part in demonstrations, and started to do regular voluntary work at feminist organisations, I went to talks, read books and articles. During the year I spent in community service, my feminist consciousness developed significantly.

Half-way through that year I decided that my way of contributing to society would be in the form of feminist work within the army. So I passed up on the roles for which I had already been selected and turned to the Chief of Staff's Adviser on Women's Affairs, which handles sexual harassment cases, among other things, asking to do my military service there. This was a phase of strong personal consciousness raising for me, and the more I became aware of feminist dilemmas, the more often, too, did I have to seriously face the issue of the army. Here I had to cope with a difficult conflict between the notions on which I had been raised from an early age — according to which the military is a positive institution and serving in it is a particularly respectable way of making your social contribution — and, on the other hand, feminist values of dignity and equality.

The army is an organisation whose most fundamental values cannot be brought into harmony with feminist values. It is a patriarchal organisation: patriarchy consists of a hierarchic social structure which is underwritten by "masculine" values such as control, a power orientation, and the repression of emotion. The army is hierarchical, and this, by definition, does not allow for equality. Indeed, the army's demand for uniformity and conformity makes it impossible for individuals to express various different identities and needs. Such a type of organisation usually undermines the weaker groups within it as well as outside it.

The army affects a society's state of mind, especially when the army takes a central role in the society. Thus, through its hierarchical nature, the army puts men in positions of power in society. The army entrenches a distorted approach to the value of equality according to which gender equality is measured in terms of the degree to which women have become included in male-identified areas of activity. An army culture of sexual harassment also spills over into civil society. Since it is a violent organisation, the army also is responsible for the increase of violence in society — and as a result, of the violence against women.

I shall look at these things in more detail below.

Women's Exclusion From Influential Positions In Society

Women in the army — in any army in the world — are relegated to the margins of power. Where the military takes a more central place, the society displays a more sexist division of roles. Women, in militarist societies, are consistently excluded from the centres of power and decision-making. Men, therefore, have an easier time than women gaining access to influential positions in a militarist society. In order to reach positions of social and political power, women have to subvert the accepted division of roles and prove themselves as against the men.

When power and influence in a society and a state are mainly under control of men, it is not only those women who want such power for themselves who suffer, but also the entire female population: decisions that affect the whole of society are made by men, according to their point of view. That is to say, usually those who make the decisions are unfamiliar with the hardships and needs of women in their society, and as a result they fail to be responsive to them, instead focusing on the problems they of know from their own experience. In fact, women as a group are weakened due to the existence of a militaristic society.

Enlistment, as far as I am concerned, means agreeing to be part of a system that is based on relations of power and control. Military service means contributing to a framework that systematically perpetuates the exclusion of women from the public sphere and construes their place in society as one that is secondary to that of men.

As a feminist it is my obligation to build civic alternatives to the army through which we can make our contribution to society, while striving, at the same time, to reduce the influence of the army on society. I cannot work, on the one hand, to support equality and recognition of the needs of various groups, while on the other hand serving a system that perpetuates the inequalities between men and women and in society at large.

The Entrenchment of Patriarchal Values and Gender Stereotypes

There is a tendency to think of women's participation in the army as a form of equality — for instance when women get to perform roles that are considered "masculine", when they are placed in combat units, or when they serve in a predominantly masculine environment. People who take this view argue that in these cases, women are not excluded from male-identified functions and/or places (this extends to the entire army as such, since it is so obviously a male institution). Women's success here, however, is actually in terms of their ability to adjust themselves to the norm of the combat soldier, the "fighting man" — a major military symbol, together with the "hero". Women, then, are expected to conform to an image which, in our culture, is powerfully identified with stereotypical masculinity. A strongly patriarchal institution, like the army, underlines female marginality, on the one hand, and the superiority of male-identified values on the other. And so, men and women who serve in the military for long periods of time undergo a process of stereotypical "gendering".

There is no doubt that gender stereotypes harm men and women alike. While the harm to women is easier to define and diagnose, as women are those who usually find themselves on the side of those who suffer from violence, humiliation and harassment, we cannot underestimate the inevitable harm caused to men, who, in order to be valued, are required — often in a non-verbal manner — to be imprisoned in a model that requires them to be oppressive, to humiliate, not to be in touch with their feelings, to act within models of "dominator and dominated" and, in extreme cases, become devoid of many attributes of human behaviour. It is impossible to prevent this disconnection, alienation, and the other elements of the emotional price that men have to pay for the constant attempt to prove "masculinity".

I do not claim that the army is solely responsible for the education for stereotypical models of femininity and masculinity, as this dichotomy is one of the pillars of any patriarchal society, and most of us internalise these messages from childhood. Yet armies, due to the fact that they are patriarchal organisations based to a large extent on stereotypical gender images, and due to the way in which they are organised, make a considerable contribution to the perpetuation of gender stereotypes.

Research has shown that women who have served in male-identified functions or in a mostly masculine environment in the military become disconnected from female-identified patterns of behaviour while at the same time internalising male-identified patterns and developing a contemptuous and aversive attitude toward other women [1]. (This proves that the army is based on "masculine" values, which are considered normative, desirable and superior in that context. And if they want to be part of such an organisation, both men and women have to accept and internalise these values: power orientation, violence, and a superior and excluding attitude to others.

If I would have to try to be part of the army this would contradict my feminist values and would require that I submit to its patriarchal values and male-identified norms. I would, thereby, support a social order which rests on power and hierarchy. I do not want to prove that I am able to serve "just like a man", I am not looking for a kind of equality that will give me rights which are the a priori privilege of men. It is absurd, in fact, to look for equality within an organisation which is fundamentally and by definition not equal, and which stands in sharp contradiction with my ideological principles and conscience.

My wish is to be a valuable member of society without subscribing to hierarchical and control-oriented principles and without being part of an organisation which is especially oppressive in its approach to women and to populations who are not included in the hegemonic group.

The Success of the Sexual Harassment Culture
Women in the army often make light of harassment, even if the sexual innuendo they have to put up with actually disturbs them. The seriousness of sexual harassment is generally played down. A patriarchal and male-dominated organisation like the army creates conditions that encourage women's sexual harassment. When women are strongly motivated to become integrated in the

66

army they may have a hard time admitting that they are exposed to harassment and that they disapprove of it. Such women are expected, to some extent, to swallow, ignore, and accept these behaviours, and even to treat them as "only natural" — as flattery, as a kind of amusing bad behavior. This is especially the case when there is no repeated approach by one particular man towards one particular woman, but rather just a certain kind of "atmosphere", something you could call "ambient sexual harassment". This consists of, for instance, certain types of remarks made by various people, songs including more or less explicit sexual hints, sexual jokes, looks, whistles, etc.

Research done in the US army has shown a strong correlation between this type of ambient sexual harassment and specific instances of personal sexual harassment [2].

And so, women in the military, especially in lower ranking functions, find themselves almost constantly oppressed and marginalised — not just because they are excluded from roles that are reserved for males only, but also because their surroundings are hostile and undermining to them as women. In fact, it might be said that a mood of sexual harassment is endemic to a patriarchal and hierarchical organization like the army.

A woman who enlists is sometimes required to cope with sexual harassment within an environment that encourages such harassment. Moreover, since the army is such a central institution in society, a culture of sexual harassment is also exported to, and further entrenched in, civil society.

This is why I, as a feminist, feel I must avoid military service and act to limit and reduce the influence of the army on civil society.

The Increase of Violence against Women in Society

Studies have shown a parallel between violence in the public sphere and considering women as inferior to men by the dominant culture [3]. In these contexts, violence against women within the family is legitimised. One explanation is that in societies that are coping with violent conflict, uses of violence within civil society become legitimised, and this, again mobilises civil society for engagement with violent military conflict. Here, the levels of violence and of indifference toward violent behaviours in all walks of life, including the family, spiral upwards. This is how violence against women ends up being tolerable and acceptable.

When men spend a formative period of their lives in the military they are likely to receive positive reinforcements for the use of brute power and violence, and to develop an indifferent attitude to the use of "mild" forms of violence, "in certain circumstances". In an organisation whose main values include superiority and control, these behaviours are likely to be encouraged in the specific professional (military) activities, but also in interpersonal relations, with regard to women and to others who are branded inferior — at home and outside, in the street.

I feel committed, as a feminist woman, to ensure women's rights in society. I cannot join an organisation, which, either directly or indirectly, encourages violence — of any form and kind — against women. Therefore there is, in my opinion, a contradiction between my being a feminist and my ability to serve in the army.

I resist being a part of the army not only on theoretical grounds. Once I understood that there is a tight connection between all the forms of women's oppression in society, I also saw that the only way for me to live as a feminist would be to watch out, wherever I was, for the social structures that make the abuse of women and other underprivileged groups possible, to oppose these and to work for their replacement with alternative values. Army service would impose a way of life on me that is deeply contrary to my values and moral beliefs. I would have to consistently deny and suppress my most fundamental persuasions. I cannot live in such flagrant denial of my conscience and I cannot serve an organisation that tramples the values on which my whole moral outlook is built.

In Israel, where there is a law that imposes army duty on Jewish men and women, there are a number of legal options through which it is possible to get an exemption from army service. As I have mentioned before, I was brought up to believe that the army was a positive and vital organisation and that serving in the army is a great contribution to society. Up to a few months before my call-up was due, I had not even considered the option of refusing to serve. The stage at which I began to think about it threw me into a sea of confusion, frustration and fears, and I felt that if I was going to avoid army service, I had to feel completely confident about what I was about to do, the reasons for it and the way in which I was about to do it.

During the period when I was thinking over the notion of refusing to serve, I felt that I had to have impeccable reasons, that I should not present an ideology that was not fully established or get an exemption in a "roundabout" way, which did not reflect my beliefs in full. Looking back, I smile at these demands that I posed to myself, as today it is clear to me that for a girl in such a confusing and complex process, both at the personal level and the social level, it is almost impossible to go through such a loaded and controversial process without any gaps. I found myself in great confusion: I felt clearly that army service collides with the values I believed in, but I knew that a feminist ideology is not an option for receiving an exemption and I found it hard to get away from the ideas I grew up with about the importance of the army and how refusing was unthinkable.

During my main period of confusion, in which I found it hard to make the link between the reason that led me to decide not to join the army and the practical ways to be discharged, I tried at first to understand what options I had. For women in Israel there are several ways to get an exemption from military service. One option that is valid for women is religious belief. I am certainly not religious, and the place where I grew up is known as quite secular. I immediately assumed that even if I tried to get an exemption for religious reasons, nobody would believe me. Another way is marriage. The thought of a marriage of convenience passed through my head, but quickly disappeared, because I didn't want to feel as though I was "cheating", and certainly didn't want to contribute to the institutions in charge of marriage in Israel, which are, to say the least, quite patriarchal and anachronistic.

The option of getting pregnant and giving birth, which also enables women to get an exemption, I did not consider seriously for one moment, for obvious reasons, so I was left with two options. One was to try to get an exemption for "psychiatric" reasons. I do believe that most people do not need to lie in order to be found mentally unsuitable for a military organisation, but I felt that such reasons did not describe in the most accurate way why I objected to military service.

The last option left to me was to apply to a military body called "The Conscience Committee". This is a military committee which is authorised to grant an exemption on grounds of conscience. In practice, the committee only approves applications that indicate that the applicant is a pacifist. Those who give their objection to the occupation as a reason, for example, do not receive an exemption, since this is seen as an objection to a specific policy employed by the government, rather than violence of any kind. Only those who claim to be pacifists and object to any kind of violence, and who would not join any army at all, can receive an exemption on grounds of conscience in Israel.

Today it is easy for me to define myself as a pacifist, but at that stage of the process I was going through I still had not defined myself as such. Again, due to those slightly exaggerated demands I posed to myself, to be completely confident without any reservations with my actions, I didn't want to apply for an exemption for reasons of pacifism.

I visualise the stage in which I ultimately decided not to enlist as an image often seen in cartoons, when a light bulb appears above a character's head. In a brief moment, entirely different from the long and constant deliberations that had occupied my mind in the preceding months, I came to a realisation. I understood that even though there was no option of applying for an exemption "on grounds of feminism", there was nothing to prevent me from doing that. It was clear to me that the feminist objection is an objection to any army, rather than a specific government policy. I do object to the occupation, but I would refuse to enlist even if it weren't for the occupation and even if it had been another country's army. Shortly afterwards I started drafting a letter for the "Conscience Committee", in which I described my feminist beliefs in detail and tried to explain in as much detail as possible the link between feminism and objection to militarism, an explanation which in the Israeli public is certainly not obvious, since "feminism" is known to the Israeli public as something completely different.

About a decade before the time when I was due to enlist, A Supreme Court case made the headlines in Israel. A young woman called Alice Miller wanted to take part in the air force training and was refused because she was a woman. In her application to the Supreme Court, backed by liberal feminist organisations, she asked the court to grant her "equality", as she interpreted the word, and asked to be given the "right" to become a military pilot, just as this right is given to men.

The only aspect seen as discriminatory in the Israeli public consciousness is the fact that women were prevented from serving in roles that were considered "masculine". The Supreme Court held that this was indeed discrimination, and the air force training became available for women too. To this day, this is considered a significant achievement, and if you ask people on the street about "army" and "feminism", there is no doubt that the name Alice Miller will be raised more than once. Therefore, it was clear to me that when I claimed that I wanted to be discharged for feminist reasons, it would raise some eyebrows, as was indeed the case.

I was put on trial in front of army representatives and sentenced to two weeks in a women's military prison. If I had any hesitations at that stage, there was no doubt that they ended at that point. Military prison reflected the oppression and the absurdity of the military system in the extreme.

After wearing the prison uniform (which belongs to the US army – rumour has it that these are the surplus of the Iraq war, which Israel received as a donation from the US army...), I joined about 50 other women of my age. Most of them were sent to prison for desertion, caused, in many cases, due to the inability of the military system to handle their problems: a soldier who escaped from her commander's sexual harassment; a girl who was a sole provider in a large family with disabled parents, who didn't receive permission from the army to work and provide for her family; a soldier who was locked in her house by a jealous partner and therefore could not arrive at the army base; and many other stories. Instead of showing understanding for their problems, the natural way in which the army handled such "useless" soldiers was by sending them to prison, which obviously didn't help in solving their problems or improving their psychological state.

The most intense experience I had in prison was the feeling of having no control. Once you arrive at the prison, most of your belongings are taken away from you, and you are put in a cell which is almost entirely full of bunk beds. You and the other prisoners have the to clean the cells each morning, but no scrubbing can remove the unbearable smell of dampness in the cells, which clings to the mattresses, the blankets, the walls, the air and you.

Most of the daily schedule in prison comprises formation parades and breaks, that are as random as can be. So you may be sitting in your cell, trying to read a book, talking to other prisoners or resting, but the moment you hear the call "60 seconds!", you must go outside immediately and form lines together with the other prisoners. The large number of formation parades, held at such short notice and at random times, contributes to the feeling of having no personal control.

When I was imprisoned, as I noticed later, my spirit of resistance and my ability to stand up for myself were undermined to some extent. I understood that the experience in which I had almost no control and no ability to make decisions about myself made me feel like a little girl who is dependent on the adults around her. Automatically, I went back to childhood patterns of behaviour, by trying to be "OK" and "not cause any trouble". One of the instances in which I realised how absurd my situation was, was when on a certain day I asked one of the officers for permission to use the public phone for more than three minutes (this is the time allocated to the prisoners' daily telephone calls. I got the permission, and the reason she gave for it was: "because you are a good soldier". I admit I didn't take that as a compliment...

If the prison experience was hard for me, I have no doubt that for those who were sent to prison as a result of personal distress — rather than the choice to refuse — this experience can be many times harder and more destructive. Eating disorders, drug abuse, sexual injuries — these are only some of the experiences of many of the prisoners. The loss of control, being disconnected from the outside world, the loneliness, the smells, and the other elements that comprise life in prison, obviously make the tough experiences even more intense.

The officers, we must remember, are girls the same age as the prisoners, who are supposed to control and supervise the prisoners and all their activities. Since they have no relevant training, I have no doubt that they don't know how to cope with the various problems that the prisoners suffer from, and I also have no doubt that they themselves may be harmed by the experience. The demand that they act in a controlling and oppressive role in such an absurd and depressing situation, in which they are told to oppress those who are in distress, raises questions that are not easy to cope with.

Spending time in prison was undoubtedly very depressing and I do not recommend it to anybody. In the Israeli refusal movement, objectors are often sent to prison repeatedly. The objector is sent to prison for several weeks for refusing to enlist, and when the first period of imprisonment ends and they persists in their refusal to enlist, they are sent to prison again and again, until one of the parties gives in: the objector (usually by deciding to get an exemption on mental grounds) or the army (usually by discharging him as a person "unsuitable" for military service, rather than as a conscientious objector). The choice to go to prison made by some of the objectors is sometimes seen as an almost heroic act in the refusal movement. You can feel the appreciation for your determination and for the willingness to sacrifice your freedom as well as your mental state, which is bound to be shaken by the imprisonment.

During my prison time, I understood the problematic aspect of the repeated imprisonment. Instead of being seen as a "heroic fighter" and being prepared to sacrifice your life and mental health for the sake of military service and fighting, you are considered as a "heroic objector", who is willing to make the sacrifices that prison entails. In my opinion, this is a duplication of a militaristic pattern of behaviour that I do not wish to be part of. Undoubtedly, sometimes there is a certain trap, because in order to voice your opinion — an ideological objection to military service — for example in the media, you are expected to perform "heroic" acts — if you haven't sacrificed you life at war, at least you've sacrificed your mental health in prison.

I reached this realisation only after entering prison and experiencing what it means, on the most emotional level. I decided that I didn't want to co-operate with the image of the "heroic objector". At the same time, the processes I went through during the period of my final encounters with the army allowed me to understand that in order to be confident with my beliefs and the reasons for my objection, I didn't need the army's seal of approval. Therefore I decided not to insist on getting an exemption as a conscientious objector.

At the end of the day, after being released from prison, and following an appeal by me and the lawyer who assisted me, I was given the dubious right to appear in front of the "Conscience Committee". The meeting with the body was an absurd experience in itself. A few days later, I had received an exemption on the grounds that I was "unsuitable for military service", backed up by the reason that "feminism" was not a reason for exemption as a conscientious objector.

One of the amusing manipulations that the "Conscience Committee" tested on me was trying to make me think that my choice to refuse to serve in the army was a choice to be "passive", as opposed to choosing an "active" way of making a change "from within".

Somehow, it is not clear to me how joining the most male chauvinistic organisation in this country can produce feminist action. It is true that in academia, in many work places, and on the street, there also exists an atmosphere of hierarchy, force or patriarchy, but only in the army is there the combination of so many oppressive elements in such an extreme manner, and only in the army are these elements vital to the essence of the organisation. A non-hierarchical, non-aggressive or non-violent army would not be an army at all; therefore it is not clear to me what "making a change from within" means. Male chauvinism does exist everywhere, but it is not a foundation stone everywhere.

The army, unlike other places with an aggressive atmosphere, needs the male chauvinist and macho values in order to exist. Without the worship of the fighting masculinity, people will start to lose interest in the combat units, which are the essence of the army. Without the repression of emotions and the admiration of superiority and aggression, people will have to develop more compassion, humanity and other characteristics that might render them unable to drop bombs into the heart of a populated area, to shoot the person standing in front of them, to humiliate entire families on a daily basis, to agree to be killed at any given time, and other routine military matters.

Another argument I encountered because of my refusal was that the army, at the end of the day, was an organisation dealing with matters of life and death, and these will always be more important than other social issues, painful as they might be. Without even entering a discussion of whether the activities of the army save lives or cause more deaths, I think this argument is based on a rather problematic perspective in the first place.

I have no doubt that in Israel there is a tendency to make the cow called the "IDF" sacred in the name of the magic word "security", and as a result, any social discourse can be silenced. Following the Second Lebanon War, the Rape Crisis Centre got many calls from women who were attacked while in the bomb shelters; in an attempt to escape the usual security threat, they found themselves exposed, without protection, to a security threat which was no less painful. I do not recall the government or society pooling their resources in order to handle the damage caused to those survivors.

Furthermore, we cannot ignore the women murdered in Israel in recent years by jealous husbands and family members, sometimes by arms belonging to "security" forces or to security companies. The characteristics of murder due to jealousy are quite familiar, and create an atmosphere of terror no less than an "external" security threat does. Nevertheless, murder within the family or between spouses is considered to be a "social" matter, of secondary importance, not a matter in which we need to invest all of our social resources — even though it is a matter of life and death, just as are the armed conflicts between different national groups.

In my act of refusal and in my life in general, I have tried to make a difference from within. Not to change the army from within, but to influence, from within, the society in which I live. I would like to live in a society which is saner, less militaristic, more equal and respectful, and less violent and oppressive. I do not think that my single act of refusal can cause all that, but I am happy to have had the strength to join a growing movement of people who are willing to ask questions.

Thanks to.Tal Hayoun for translation from Hebrew to English

Footnotes

[1] Sason-Levy, Orna 2003 "Feminism and military gender practices: Israeli Women Soldiers in 'Masculine' Roles. The sociological Inquiry vol. 73, No. 3, pp 440-465

[2] Firestone, Juanita M., and Harris, Richard J., "Sexual Harassment in the U.S. Military: Individualized and Environmental Contexts", Armed Forces & Society, Vol. 21, No. 1, Fall 1994

[3] Schmeidl, S. and E Piza-Lopez (2002). Gender and Conflict Early Warning: A Framework for Action, International Alert and the Swiss Peace Foundation.

Eritrean Women: In a Crossfire between Conscription and Denial of Conscientious Objector Status

Eritrea is located in the Horn of Africa, and won its independence from Ethiopia after 30 years of a bitter, bloody and costly armed struggle. The war of independence started in 1961 and Eritrea formally declared independence on 24 May 1993, after an overwhelming yes vote in a referendum overseen by the United Nations.

Eritrea is one of only two countries in the world which has conscription of women. The government has militarised the country completely. Forced recruitment of young people, underage children, and adults under 50 is a daily event. Recruits are treated brutally and there is evidence of sexual abuse of women. Nobody has a right to question the military authorities. Nobody has a right to conscientious objection. Conscientious objectors are branded by the regime as cowardly and unpatriotic. There is no recourse to the law, nor substitute civilian service for conscientious objectors. The consequences of conscientious objection and desertion are severe torture, long-term imprisonment and even death.

The number of conscientious objectors within the military increased after the border war with Ethiopia in 1998-2000. Today there are thousands who objected to military service. They are forced to go into exile. Considerable numbers of them are seeking political asylum in Europe, especially Germany, Libya, Ethiopia, Egypt, Israel and Sudan. In Germany, Eritrean refugees founded the *Eritrean Antimilitarism Initiative* (EAI) which supports refugees and works to promote peace and antimilitarism in Eritrea.

Due to the excessive abuses and violation of human rights against women by the military, the number of women who have tried to leave their country has been high. *Ruta Yosef-Tudla* and *Bisrat Habte Micael* are two young women who are courageous enough to tell their experiences to the public. Ruta is a pacifist and fled before she was drafted. Bisrat tells her story from the perspective of her compulsory national service, before she managed to flee. They are now living in Germany.

There is no human rights organisation to campaign against the abuses suffered by conscripts. The *Eritrean Women's Association* has been part of the regime and shows little concern, or is not allowed even, to investigate rapes and other sexual abuses in the military.

It is believed that one in four of the fighters in the army is a woman. The National Service Proclamation in 1994 by the present government obliges women to undertake national service. According to the proclamation, all women and men over 18 are required to do six months of military training and a year of work on national reconstruction. After the proclamation, the opposition to women's participation came particularly from the Muslim communities for religious reasons. It has been reported that in some lowland areas, where the concentration of Muslims is high, the government was not implementing the proclamation in the same way as in the highlands.

After the border war with Ethiopia, the section of the proclamation limiting the duration of service to 18 months has not been followed. The most affected group have been women, whose length of service became lenghtened by an unlimited amount.

In the past few years, the Sawa training camp has been established as the headquarters for universal national service. All high school students, female and male, are forced to finish their last of 12 years of study in a school within Sawa. None of them has returned for further education at university once they completed national service. Only very few of them were transferred to the new colleges like Mai NefHi and other semi-military colleges which started after the University of Asmara, Eritrea's only such institution, was closed by the government. The new colleges are administered by military officers.

Until the war of independence, Eritrea was a very traditional and patriarchal society, although things have been changing in recent years, especially in the cities. Legally and theoretically women are equal to men. In general the right to an education is free for everybody. Women who are educated have a higher status in society. They have equal opportunity in work. In the cities they can decide their own life in marriage and other social areas. They can participate in politics and other fields which were dominated by men. But due to the long tradition of male dominance, their full participation in and protection by society is still at its earliest stage.

Both the highland Christian areas and lowland Muslim areas are conservative in attitudes towards women. The father or the eldest boy is the boss of the house. If they are not there, the uncles and male relatives have power over women and girls. Women are restricted to domestic affairs like childcare and running the house. Men decide on all aspects of the social and economic life of the family, including whom the daughters should marry. Until recently, only men played a political role in the villages. Only men were judges, government officials and other functionaries. Only men were Elders, who do some arbitration and mediation in the villages.

Arming Eritrean women started during the struggle for independence. Both the *Eritrean People's Liberation Front* (EPLF) and the *Eritrean Liberation Front* (ELF) encouraged women to become active fighters. The EPLF in particular represented this goal as part of their promotion of equality for women.

After independence National Service included and legalised women as part of the military service. Some scholars argue that the participation of women during the war for independence helped to break down the dominance of males. They point out that the status of women did get better. They got political power. There were some women appointed as ministers and to other important posts. Moreover, the first constitution of 1997 made clear the equality of women. The document reserved 30 per cent of parliamentary seats for women, apart from those who had been elected. However, the position of ordinary women largely remained as before, with all its harshest elements, especially for those in national service.

After independence, the EPLF immediately established a transitional government with all administrative posts and other key positions filled by EPLF members. At its third congress in 1994, the EPLF renamed itself the *Peoples Front for Democracy and Justice* (PFDJ). Unlike its name, the regime was undemocratic and unjust as well as unconstitutional. In September 2001 the PFDJ crushed all opposition to it, ignoring the constitution that had been ratified in 1997.

Today the PFDJ is a ruthless dictatorship, the sole lawmaker. Eritreans are denied their basic civil and human rights, any protests always ending in arbitrary arrest, detention and torture. For all Eritreans whose vision of their new nation included peace, stability and prosperity, the scale of wars, corruption and abuse of power that followed independence was unbelievable. Eritrea today is a country where poverty and oppression are the rule. There are no independent newspapers or TV channels and all sources of information are coloured by government propaganda.

Here, then, are Ruta's and Bisrat's stories in their own words. Their statements have been edited for the purpose of this anthology.

Introduction by Ellen Elster and Abraham G Mehreteab. A different version of this introduction appeared in The Broken Rifle No 68, November 2005.

Ruta Yosef-Tudla: "I'm Against War on Principle."

I was born on 27 November 1987 in Asmara and grew up with my four siblings. My mother died in 1996. In the same year, my father was arrested and imprisoned without explanation. After my mother had died, my grandmother on the mother's side took care of us and I had to help her. After she also died in 2001, my grandmother on the father's side came to us. She comes from a village. So I had to assist her and could not go to school. In 2003 I had to interrupt schooling.

I did very badly in Eritrea. Twice a week we had to attend military training for two to three hours in school. Sometimes we did a long march or had training in the school. Schoolgirls were also brought to Gahtelay, where it is really hot and where you can die from thirst. Two of my classmates died there.

Especially during the war, almost all teenage students were conscripted compulsorily and taken to Sawa and to the frontline. Some were killed in action, some suffered injuries and are now disabled. Some also came back and were allowed to finish school. May 24 is the day of liberation. This day is popularly celebrated. On television it was shown that all teenagers celebrate independence and performed well drilled exercises. Three months before the independence celebration, teenagers were therefore taken from school. Whoever did anything wrong was beaten. Once, even the parents protested against it. They said that their children were not allowed to attend school. Mothers bravely demonstrated although they were not allowed to. They said:

"Our girls are kept from their education. So they will be regarded badly in society. Therefore they should continue school and should be left to study again. If they have to practise something similar [to military training], then it should only on a voluntary basis."

Because the mothers had demonstrated, they were regarded as opponents of independence. Some of them were arrested. There is no freedom of speech. There is no religious freedom either. Especially for women the situation is difficult. Some were taken forcefully to Sawa for basic training. There they were treated like slaves and also raped. Christians became pregnant from Muslims and vice versa. Some were disowned by their families. The women could hardly endure all this. So some killed themselves, others their child, and some became crazy. Those who can live in Eritrea without problems belong to families of executives or people who have a lot of money. The children of the rulers, of the generals, of the officials and of other high-ranking people, are protected from conscription. All others must die in the war. In my eyes, this is not correct. All this has deterred and scared me.

Because I had interrupted school [to help at home], I wasn't allowed back into school again. Instead, I faced being forced to undertake national service. Some teenagers were even recruited forcefully on the street. So the time came that I would have been called up for national service. I was clear in my mind that I didn't want to do it for several reasons. One is that I am softhearted by nature. I was also educated religiously so that it would be a sin for me to participate in war. Furthermore I am against war on principle. I don't know at all why war is waged. Who dies and who's in a safe place? The rulers, the members of their families and their children are in a safe place. The others must die. Is there a meaningful war at all? War results in dead people and poverty. The children suffer from it.

Another reason is that two of my siblings had been called up for the war and we didn't ever get any message from them. Another reason was that my father was arrested without any explanation. They took him when we were not at home. Later the soldiers came once again in order to search the house. Then I asked them: "Why did you arrest him? Where is my father?" Instead of answering me, I was beaten. So far, we don't know where our father remains.

So I was in a difficult situation because of the threat of conscription. A friend of my father promised to help me to get out of the country. I was able to go with him to Sudan in the year 2003. I didn't remain long in Sudan, just for one or two months. I don't feel well since I came to Germany. I live in a small village, Seeheim-Jugenheim, near Darmstadt. I have difficulties with the social welfare office. I am not allowed to visit my friends or family. I had applied to be resettled in new accommodation. It was also agreed that I could move to relatives. But my application was finally rejected. Now, I am often not in the camp. Therefore, welfare services have been reduced several times.

Ruta Yosef-Tedla was interviewed on 2 June 2004. Translation by Axel Heinemann. The German version was published in: Connection e.V. (editor) Offenbach, Germany: Eritrea: Kriegsdienstverweigerung und Desertion, November 2004.

Bisrat Habte Micael: "I've Had Enough of the War."

I was born on 10 January 1981 in Asmara. I finished the grade 11 and took my school leaving examinations, I was just 15 years old. We were told that we would get the results of the school leaving examinations only after basic training in National Service. That's why at the age of 15 I joined the military, hoping that my exam results were good and I could leave, after basic training, to study. Thus in 1996 I was recruited for National Service as part of the fifth recruitment round and taken to Sawa for basic training.

The time in Sawa was hard. It was the rainy season and the facilities at Sawa were poor at that time. Many became ill, and got hepatitis. Women especially frequently got hiccups; we call this lewti. Even when ill we were forced to take part in the roll-call. Only when you were very seriously ill was it possible to get a postponement from National Service. We were forced to take part in military exercises until we were completely exhausted. They did not care whether you would die or not. Relatives of high ranking officers were treated differently. They got exempted from military service even without being ill.

Many girls were raped. There were girls who adapted themselves to the situation and made advances to officers out of their own initiative, to avoid being raped. There were only male officers. Girls who didn't comply, who rejected the men, were given the worst work or sent into the war. The girls who had been raped but didn't want to comply were sent to the front. The girls who were compliant and pretty were treated well. Often they got pregnant without wanting to.

After six month of basic training I came to the 381st division. First I was supposed to work in administration, but then I was sent to the front line. This surprised me. I assumed that I would serve a total of 18 month of military service. After deducting holidays, this would have meant 8 months after the end of basic training, which the soldiers usually serve. I also had applied for holidays. But my superior wanted to prevent me from doing this. He wanted me to cook for him and to be his puppet. I refused that.

Girls who refused to play the housewife had to stand on guard service for 3 to 4 hours at night as a form of punishment. Young men who wanted to help them were punished too. They were ordered to stand at attention in the sun for an entire day. The other girls, who played along with the game, were treated well. They got a good room, a nice bed, and got holidays every month to visit their families. But very few played along. Most refused. We always thought: we would do military service and then go back home.

After serving 18 months in military service, we had to stay on for two additional months. Then the war began. It is difficult for me to describe this. It was horrible. For example, five or six young soldiers died and they had just been left in the field. When the unit withdrew from the front for a break, some went to their families without authorisation. When they returned and the unit had been sent back to the front, these soldiers were sent directly to the front as a form of punishment. Others were even executed. I have had enough of the war. I reported ill, although that meant I had to stay there and couldn't go home. After several requests and complaints I finally got five days of holidays, but I stayed away for 10 days. Then I got very scared. I returned. As punishment I had to carry a big water container up and down a hill for a full week.

In May 1999 the unit commander tried to rape me. I screamed and others came to help me and prevented it from happening. I demanded that he be punished, but it was his responsibility to pass on my complaint to his superiors. He did not get punished. Later my superior put me under pressure and told lies about me, because I did not comply to his demands. For example, he accused me of stealing some money, although he didn't leave any money around. He passed on this kind of accusations to his superiors, so that I would be punished. It was unbearable. Therefore I went to my family in Asmara. After one month I was arrested, and was brought to the police station in Gegjeret. After that I was sent to Adiabeto. I demanded repeatedly: "*I want to be brought to my unit. If I am to get punished, then I want to get punished there.*"

After some weeks I was able to escape from the prison in Adiabeto and went to Adisegdo. I managed to stay there for more than a year and had to hide all the time. Because I had been gone for a long time, the authorities put pressure on my father, and finally arrested him. With the help of his friends, I was finally able to flee to Sudan. There I stayed for one week to prepare the rest of my flight.

In Sudan too I feared to be arrested. The Eritrean president Afewerki had given orders to arrest deserters and to bring them back to Eritrea. The Eritrean government demanded that young people who had fled to Sudan to be handed over. Sometimes the Sudanese government complied with this request and deported young people to Eritrea. Some of the deserters were shot, some simply disappeared. Also the Eritrean Secret Service is active in Sudan, and sometimes kidnaps Eritrean secret carriers, but also common soldiers. In addition, the Sudanese soldiers, for example in Kessela, are corrupt. Because of the conflicts between Sudan and Eritrea, they do not care what happens to deserters. Those who won't give them money are arrested and brought back to the border. Deserters can't even expect help from the United Nations.

In Sudan I stayed for one month with a relative in Khartoum. With his help and the help of people smugglers I was able to get to Germany. Here in Germany I am fine. I have found rest. My application for asylum, however, has been turned down by the authorities. I am appealing against the decision, but I don't have much hope. I don't know how my family is doing, and I am really worried. I cannot phone them or write, because they are probably watched. I am scared that my family might get even deeper into trouble if the authorities knew that they had helped me. I don't have any information about my father. I do not know if he is still alive. My siblings have been called up for National Service. My mother is on her own. I do not know how they can bear it.

Bisrat Habte Micael was interviewed on 28 May 2004, Translation from Tigri into German by Yonas Bahta and Abraham Gebreyesus. Translation from German to English by Andreas Speck. Source: Connection e.V./Eritreische Antimilitaristische Initiative: Dokumentation: Eritrea: Kriegsdienstverweigerung und Desertion

Women from the US Resist War in the Gulf, Afghanistan and Iraq

onscription of men ended in 1973 in the USA., which now has an all-volunteer military. A well-funded system is used to convince young people to join. Annual funding for recruiting and retention programs more than doubled from 2003 to 2007, from US$3.4 billion to US$7.7 billion. Presently women make up about 15% of the military, nearly a half a million of the 3 million soldiers in the combined Armed Forces; 11% of the total force deployed to Iraq and Afghanistan is women [1]. Although women are officially banned from combat duty (a policy that the military uses to recruit women), the reality is that every position in wars such as Iraq and Afghanistan is a combat position.

There are many reasons women go into the military. *Stephanie Atkinson* and *Tina Garnanez*, while they enlisted almost 20 years apart from each other, both write of coming from low-income families with few opportunities and being unclear about what they wanted to do. These young people are easy targets for military recruiters.

Anita Cole and *Diedra Cobb*, who had both gone to college before entering, wrote that they believed going into the military was a way to serve their country and *"sacrifice for the greater good"*, a theme promoted in ads for the military.

Each of the women had to make a difficult decision as their opposition to war grew. *Katherine Jashinski*'s statement reflects what they all decided when she said, *"I will not compromise my beliefs for any reason."* There were consequences to their varied actions.

Stephanie Atkinson and *Diedra Cobb* were both asked to write for this anthology, which they found painful to do. Stephanie said, *"I struggle considerably to tell the story of my experience."* *"Sometimes I don't know if want to revisit this story again"*, wrote Diedra. For Diedra that includes mentioning that she was sexually assaulted in the barracks. Rape is a serious threat to women in the military. Government surveys have shown that almost a third of women in the military are sexually assaulted.

Both of them are clear how difficult it is to be questioning the military while in it. As Stephanie tells us, *"It would be years after my resistance that I began to educate myself and be able to understand intellectually what I only felt ill-at-ease with."* She points to *Cynthia Enloe*'s writings as a good source of information on nationalism and masculinity from a feminist perspective. Stephanie was asked if she could write more about that, but she felt that was another chapter that she couldn't do for this book. However, she did talk about what she called the *"hyper-*

masculinized culture of the military." The message to women in the military, she explained, is: *"I will allow you to be here but you will always be the Other."* There is a level of femininity that is non-threatening to this culture, but not all women fit that.

An August 2008 Government Accountability Office Report found that the military's efforts to combat sexual violence had been hampered by a lack of support from some senior commanders. Many women in the military report that there is a high incidents of sexual assault by higher ranking men and commanders.

"The Pentagon's latest figures show that nearly 3,000 women were sexually assaulted in fiscal year 2008, up 9% from the year before; among women serving in Iraq and Afghanistan, the number rose by 25%. When you look at the entire universe of female victims, close to a third say they were victims of rape or assault while they were serving — twice the rate of the civilian population." [2]

A woman who experienced such abuse was unable to write about it, although she tried. *Jessica* (who prefers her surname not be used) first told her story publicly at a vigil for gays and lesbians who had been victims of violence. Most of the stories told that night were about others, people who did not survive the homophobic abuse. But Jessica told her own story. When she was in the military she had gone to a gay bar, went out for air, and was kidnapped and raped by her drill sergeants, strangled and left for dead. High school students who were actively involved in countering military recruitment at their school asked her to talk to their YouthPeace group, which she did.

Jessica went into the military in her early twenties, having worked as a personal fitness trainer. She was physically strong, and therefore threatening to the men in the military. Jessica was harassed from the the beginning of Basic Training. She told how she survived the rape and strangulation, how documents regarding the incident were stolen from her locker and she was sent to another base to go back through basic training. Jessica suffered Post Traumatic Stress Disorder which was not treated in the military. Jessica was targeted because, as Stephanie described, she did not meet the hyper-masculinized military culture's *"level of femininity"*. After a year of horrendous abuse Jessica was able to leave the military with money that allowed her to go to college and get the help she needs for the Post Traumatic Stress Disorder. But Jessica found it too painful to write her story. She hopes that she will some day be able to, but needs to give herself more time to heal.

In this section you will read about women who enlisted in the military over a 20-year period, from those who were faced with the first Gulf War, to the wars in Iraq and Afghanistan. They tell of the changes they experienced during basic training, as they were influenced by what they read, learned about the US role in the world, were given weapons, and confronted the reality of war and killing. While they each have their own story of how they came to oppose war, and how they left the military, there are similarities in their experiences that are shared by many others whose stories have not been told.

Introduction by Joanne Sheehan, War Resisters League

Footnotes

[1] Budget figures: The Washington Post, May 11, 2009. All figures of numbers in the military from US Department of Defense, 2009
[2] The War Within by Nancy Gibbs, Time Magazine, March 8, 2010

A Proud Deserter

By Stephanie Atkinson

I am not a conscientious objector. I am not someone who has had to defend my beliefs for not participating in war. I am someone who when called upon to participate in a war that I thought was unjustifiable for many reasons, refused to go. I went AWOL (absent without leave) from the US Army in opposition to Operation Desert Storm. I am only a small part of a long continuum of war resisters, but I am proud of the decision I made to refuse.

If you are legally accepted as a conscientious objector by the US military, you are dismissed honorably. But conscientious objectors have gone through a very difficult and formal military process in which they have defended their actions, usually based on religious or strongly moral opposition to war. I define myself as a war resister for many reasons: I never submitted an application for conscientious objector status, and if I had, I don't think that I would have been able to defend my opposition. My reasons for refusal were predominantly political, and murky at best. I think of myself as a proud deserter. I think there are a lot of people who are like me, maybe not so proud, but definitely deserters or people who go AWOL, who may not have solidly defined reasons, but do have a cumulative set of experiences and feelings that add up to a feeling of "*not quite right*".

I struggle considerably to tell the story of my experience. I have no noble sense of opposition based on deeply held religious beliefs, as I'm not a religious person. At the time of my resistance, I had no eloquent or well-reasoned argument based on research or political study. (That education came later, substantiating and validating my feelings.) I did however, have feelings and experiences that indicated to me that my participation in the first Gulf War would be wrong. I was not swayed by the arguments of loyalty or patriotism, and going AWOL wasn't a moral or amoral dilemma to me that had to be justified by a religious or moral reason. I did not feel the pressure of *"my country right or wrong"*. In fact, I felt something completely opposite: *"This is wrong, for a multitude of reasons, and I'm not going to do it. People on both sides will die, money and resources will be wasted, nothing about this will do anything to advance the human condition."*

My Way into the US Army

I enlisted in the US Army reserves at the age of seventeen in September of 1984 with my mother's permission. It was a very quick and casual decision. I had no plans to enlist at that age; I had very little plans at all. Although I was an honor student in high school I didn't have much guidance. My home life was emotionally and financially troubled. In my senior year of high school, I began easing my way out of home with only murky ideas about my future. I had dropped out of all extracurricular activities, started working part-time jobs, and only going to school half a day. More than anything I wanted to be independent, responsible for myself financially, and move on with my life.

I grew up in small town America. There are many communities like the one I grew up in — agrarian and working class, politically and religiously conservative, and with limited economic opportunities. (Later when I met other resisters, a lot of us shared similarities of circumstance, whether we were from rust belt cities, small towns or inner cities. A lot of us came from single parent working class households. Most commonly we didn't quite know who we wanted to be or what we wanted to do. And really, at 17, 18 or 21 years old, who does?)

These are ideal communities for recruiting young people to the military. For young adults without defined life paths, the military is presented as an opportunity up and out of their present circumstances, to a college education, steady employment, financial independence, travel, experiences that they wouldn't have if they stayed in their communities. With my good grades, earnestness and naïveté, and fierce desire to leave home, I was an ideal candidate.

On a visit to a recruiting station with my stepfather (who wanted to enlist in the Navy) and mother, I was an easy mark. I had taken the ASVAB (Armed Services Vocational Aptitude Battery) because I enjoyed standardized tests in high school. Conveniently, my scores were available to the recruiter in the office. I was bright, healthy, young, with no plans for the future and an enthusiastic parent who would sign the age waiver for enlistment immediately. I could learn valuable job skills! Travel the world! Get a college education! The recruiters reinforced for my mother and me everything we wanted to hear to make enlistment appealing, and didn't dissuade us from any misinformed perceptions about what being in the military really meant. Within a couple of hours, my preliminary enlistment was done. I remember feeling really excited, a little nervous, but that I had something to look forward to in less than a year. I had made a grown up decision and was close to becoming an independent adult. I was swirling in a haze of deceptive daydreams. I was a teenager with limited information who had made a very adult decision certainly, one of life and death. The remotest thing I had considered was that being in the US Army meant one very concrete thing — War. I had no particularly strong feelings or information about world or national events or even feelings of patriotism or "a higher calling". I had never considered war or violence other than as a part of "ancient history". Both my grandfathers had served in World War II, but that was the stuff of "old people". Like most other teenagers I had no sense of mortality or concern for the world at large, only changing my own immediate circumstances. Is that selfish? Yes. Is it uncharacteristic of most young people? No.

The misperceptions of my decision to enlist were quickly adjusted during the reality of basic training in the summer of 1985. The fundamental mission of basic training is to create soldiers — to break down psychically, emotionally, physically the person one was before and remold her into a *"lean mean fighting machine"*. The transformation from naive teenager to soldier was difficult for me. Even in the emotionally troubled household I had grown up in, I was accustomed to yelling and flaring tempers. This was the first time however, that being *"good"* or *"smart"* wasn't a characteristic I could rely on to avoid being yelled at. Every day I asked to go home, every day, I was denied. It was pretty obvious from early on that I was a mismatch for the military. I kept hoping I could fail my way out of basic training. The funny thing though was that I became leaner, meaner, stronger and someone valuable to retain. My drill sergeant threatened me with *"recycling"* which meant repeating basic training again, rather than graduating and moving on to advanced individual training. Being recycled was the worst possible thing I could think of and an impetus for me to try harder each day to get through.

Gradually I started to get into my training. Sleep deprivation, the change in diet, constant group contact, change in living circumstances, and training, will wear a person down. But even then war was an abstraction. The drills, training with weapons, simulations and field exercises were still not within a context of meaning. This was just something I had to *"get through"*. By mid October of 1985 I had completed basic training and advanced individual training at Ft Jackson, South Carolina. In November and December, I came home and stayed there, retreated. It took my mother's encouragement for me to enroll in the spring semester of college. The naive teenage girl I had been died. I was a changed person — harder, more fearful and cautious around others. Before military training, I was excited about trying new things, now I became reluctant for fear that if I didn't feel safe, I wouldn't be able to change my mind.

Growing Resistance

Like most young Americans, I didn't have the interest or time to pay attention to the world and its events. Since the difficult part of my military training was over, being a reservist one weekend a month and two weeks in the summer was just another job for me. I soon adjusted to the liberties and responsibilities of being a college student. I worked multiple part time jobs, carried at least a full semester course load and tried to eke out a better life for myself even as I was committed to a 6-year contract with the US Army. Along the way, I tried to have some fun, make friends, and enjoy living as independently as I'd always wanted.

It wasn't difficult to feel like the reservist soldier part of my life wasn't significant to the rest of my existence and war certainly wasn't a reality. The Vietnam War was an old issue that belonged to my parents' generation, something discussed in history classes. In the mid 80s of the Reagan era, military conflicts were relegated to jungles in small Spanish-speaking countries or dismantling walls and ending cold wars. But still I kept noticing disturbing trends. It seemed like every holiday season, the US was invading another country. I remember feeling anxiety when the US invaded Panama.

Soon my experiences learning about the world and my role in it dovetailed with my experiences as a *"part time"* soldier. Between 1987 and 1989, I took two trips abroad, one to Japan, and one to South Korea as part of Operation Team Spirit, an annual joint military exercise. I became increasingly ill at ease with how we as individual people conducted ourselves outside of our country, behaving as the *"ugly Americans"*. I was frustrated by our lack of concern for the people and landscape who served as our hosts. These were the people who were working with us to defend our mutual interests and we treated them so poorly. These were my experiences on a personal level, not a global one. It would be years after my resistance that I began to educate myself and be able to understand intellectually what I only felt ill at ease with. (Scholars such as Cynthia Enloe, in her work *Bananas, Beaches and Bases*, eloquently explain the impact of a military base's influence on a community and ultimately its country [1].) My experiences were limited to accompanying friends in my unit to nightclubs and strip shows, getting drunk and trying to keep them out of fights, and otherwise behaving badly.

Meanwhile as a student, in my *"real life"*, I started hanging out with friends in the small counterculture of Southern Illinois University, the punk rockers who wrote 'zines about music and politics. We participated in protests against nuclear weapons and really started to pay attention to events emerging in the Reagan era like Iran-Contra. My participation in my reserve unit became an irritation that I had to put up with. (I'm sure the feeling was mutual with my command.) I was becoming increasingly disobedient, irascible, and not behaving as a *"team player"*. I was essentially playing a waiting game, trying to expend the minimum amount of effort required to participate. I was a really lousy soldier. I would come to weekend drills with punk rock haircuts, refuse to qualify with my weapon on the firing ranges, and otherwise nurse a bad attitude. Some of this I attribute to being a young person, but also to my growing discontent with a long-term commitment to being a soldier. After all, being in the Army wasn't a job I could just *"quit"*. I wish I had known that there were military counselors who could help people like me.

In my final summer camp of 1990, I was looking forward to the end of my 6-year contract. I was 23, less than a year out of college and ready to move on. I still didn't know what I wanted to do with my life, but I was pretty clear that I didn't want to continue being part of the Army. It had been a mismatched relationship from the beginning exacerbated by my experiences and education. I was at this final summer camp in Wisconsin with another unit because I had missed my unit's summer camp. On the final day of the military exercise, I had learned that Iraq had invaded Kuwait. Again, this event seemed like it had no relationship to my reality, I would be out of the reserves in a month. I had outlasted the waiting game.

Activated for Service

When I was activated for service in October of 1990, I was stunned and frustrated that what I thought was my end of service really had no end. President George H W Bush had signed a *"Stop Loss"* order meaning that no service personnel would be released from duty, there would be no attrition, no loss, as early as August of 1990 (even though the US wouldn't invade Iraq until January of 1991).

Frankly, my desires for my future, concerns, misgivings, and confusion about my military experience and the world political stage were of no concern to the army, my moral ambiguities about the meaning of war were irrelevant. I was just one person who was part of a very large operation, the time to *"quit"* or be *"fired"* for poor performance had past.

When my unit was initially put on alert status, I made preparations as if to go. I felt like I had no choice. Soon after, I read about two conscientious objectors, Jeff Paterson and Erik Larsen. Both of them were Marines and after reading accounts of their opposition to war, something resonated in me, *"I'm like that"*, although I hadn't the ability to articulate what *"that"* was. Paterson had sat down on the tarmac at Kaneohe Air Station in Hawaii, the photos of him showed a skinny Buddha in fatigues, immovable. Larsen's writings and speeches were a checklist of concise reasons to oppose war and violence on both religious and political grounds. Both of these men demonstrated bravery in refusal, in saying *"no"*, in the quiet act of sitting down or simply saying *"I am no longer a Marine"*. I felt that I, too, could quit.

I decided that I would change my plans. Rather than reporting for duty, ready to ship to Kuwait, I would report for duty, ready to turn myself in and refuse service.

I received lots of bad advice from well intentioned people during this time, suggestions to become pregnant, declare myself a homosexual (in the pre-Clinton *"don't ask don't tell"* days it would be grounds for dismissal), suggestions that were unacceptable if I was taking responsibility for my beliefs and feelings. I had seen the example of Paterson and Larsen and felt that I should identify myself as a resister and face the consequences. I wasn't really sure what the consequences would be, but I felt that facing them would be the better choice than going to war or lying about my reasons. At some point I made a simple decision, I would rather spend time in jail than go to the impending Gulf War. I had no idea how long I could go or where to, but it just seemed simple. War wasn't an option. Of all the things a person can do and come to regret later, there is no way one can undo perpetrating violence and perhaps killing another human being.

Public Refusal

I contacted a group I had read about, Citizen Soldier, who encouraged me to go public with my situation and file for conscientious objector status, rather than report for duty to pre-emptively turn myself in. I was inadequately prepared for what this would mean, but the publicity of my case played a significant role in determining the outcome. Tod Ensign of Citizen Soldier is a very skilled advocate for soldiers and veterans who had a long history of organizing and working with the media. He and attorney Louis Font, a conscientious objector of the Vietnam War, took on my case. I spoke out publicly at events and was interviewed on television. I was very bad at being my own advocate, with very little media savvy. I was also legally AWOL and so my application for conscientious objector status, had I even filed one, would have been moot. The formal procedure to being declared a conscientious objector is not an easy one. The soldier must make an application, undergo evaluations by experts to determine sincerity of conviction and while waiting determination of status fully participate under order of one's command. Being activated for duty and refusing to report to my unit immediately undermined any consideration for my case as a conscientious objector. It is for this reason that I think of myself as a war resister.

The way my resistance played out in the public arena is both a blessing and a curse. On a positive side, because I was so very public in the early build up to the war, I think the army wanted to shut me up and be rid of me quickly to avoid a morale incident that would affect other troops. From a public relations standpoint, one person against a very large credibly regarded organization is an easy battle. I would be treated as an aberration, not representative of the army and its soldiers, a one-off, a mistake. (This resulted in my fairly quick release.) My resistance enraged those who didn't support me, but also earned the trust and help of a small group of people who sympathized and supported me. I was confused and frightened by the reaction of people I didn't know to my decision. It seemed unsettling to me that my very personal decision for which I would suffer the consequences would cause such public controversy. I was flabbergasted that anyone would really care about my personal opposition to the war. Members of my unit who I considered friends weren't really surprised nor were most of my friends at the university. But still residing where I did, the backlash and anger at being so nonconformist in a traditional community really ended the life I knew there. I received threats by phone and mail and didn't feel safe as a *"fugitive"*.

Arrested and Discharged from the Army

I was arrested in late October, on a Friday evening at home. A state trooper served a warrant at my house and took me to the county jail. Shortly thereafter, I was picked up by a military police unit from Scott Air Force Base and held over the weekend. Eventually, I was transferred to Fort Knox personnel confinement facility in Kentucky while waiting for charges. The facility wasn't really jail, but a temporary barracks for other people awaiting discharge ... bad apples who had run afoul of the Uniform Code of Military Justice. This would be my last experience in the Army, similar to basic training: uncertain about the outcome of my future, separated from everything I knew. After a couple of weeks, I was offered an administrative separation under *"Other than Honorable Conditions"* from the Army. My rank would be busted down to E-1, I wouldn't receive veterans' benefits, I wouldn't be buried with a flag on my coffin and I was forbidden to enlist again. This was all fine with me. I would be happy to end the relationship. I was a very fortunate person. Even as my unit was just settling in at Kuwait, I was no longer a member of the army.

Even before the war started in January of 1991, my life was completely different. I couldn't just pick up where my life had left off before. I worked at a small business but had to leave the job when the boss explained to me that people in the community threatened to withdraw their business if I continued in his employ. After having received threats by phone and mail, I was constantly paranoid whenever I felt someone looking at me *"funny"*. Neighbors and people who I thought had been friends weren't so friendly anymore, even some extended family didn't really know how to interact with me. I was very fortunate that I was soon offered the Jim Bristol Fellowship at the Youth & Militarism Program of the American Friends Service Committee in Philadelphia, PA. Harold Jordan, the director of the Youth & Militarism Program had been an early advocate and provided a concrete opportunity for me to take my experience and apply it to a positive direction. From there I met people who supported me, who were conscientious objectors and war resisters from previous eras. An especially active group who took others and me under their wing during this time was Veterans for Peace. I was befriended by a woman named Nancy Clarke, a member of the very active Boston Veterans for Peace group.

A Community of War Resisters

For war resisters who have come to reject participation in war, we all arrived at the same decision but through such different circumstances that no two stories are the same. The consequences of our experiences however, are universal: knowing that somehow we are different, *"other"*; the sense of isolation we initially feel; the ostracism from our peers, strangers and even loved ones for articulating our difference. That feeling occurs before one initiates a request to be recognized as a conscientious objector or decides to desert. Becoming a war resister or conscientious objector isn't a decision that one makes suddenly, it occurs as the tipping point of accumulated experience. Even when pressed to articulate this *"a-ha!"* moment, some of us struggle, others are eloquent, but we are together in our refusal.

The only true thing I can tell war resisters and conscientious objectors is this: It's okay to be scared of the consequences. We live in a scary world. Not everyone will understand or support you, some people may threaten you and you may spend time in jail. But other people will support you. There's a whole community of people who believe that what you are doing is right. It's okay to not be able to fully articulate your reasons for why you think your participation in war is wrong. You don't have to solve the conflicts or propose a diplomatic solution to the problem just because you think war is wrong. You don't have to have all the answers. No matter what the outcome, hold in your heart — for the rest of your — life, confidence in your decision. You did the right thing.

Footnotes

[1] Cynthia Enloe: Making Feminist sense of international politics. Bananas, beaches and bases. London, Sydney, Wellington, Pandora 1989

The Power of Telling One's Story

By Diedra Cobb

Dear God, please hear me. I need to hear my spirit guides. I need to quiet my mind chatter. I need to soar like the Goddess that I am. I need to write. I need to create. I need to build with myself and with others. I need to have fun. I need to eat well. I need loving, attentive affection. I need strong, loving, focused, affirmative community. I need my femininity to be honored. I need the trees and the water. I need straight forward and productive communication with those around me and beyond. I need Mother Nature's strength and guidance. I need the truth. I need you. I need myself. Thank you. I love you. I love me.

Sacrifice for the Greater Good

Sometimes I don't know if I want to visit this story again. The experience of writing this story represents the psychosis of my interactions with this society as a woman, as a black woman, as a thinker, as a spiritual being. Telling this story represents reliving, reawakening, re-evaluating, re-envisioning, renewing what has been all along — creation. Knowing that telling this story is what I need, trying to be thorough, knowing that I will probably fall short of my most critical expectations, and knowing that everything is in balance — always — I write. Little by little I tell my story to myself. Little by little I tell my story to others. And little by little I heal, I gain clarity, and I love my beautiful self unconditionally, so that I can love others unconditionally.

I began my journey with the military in June 2001. I joined the Army Reserves with the understanding that I was uniting with a community of people that believed in sacrifice for the greater good. I joined the Army Reserves with the understanding that I would be building safe and more free futures for my fellow humans, whether near or far, and with that understanding, I felt invigorated and alive.

My father and uncle had served in the military, and in my interactions with them then and now, never would I characterize them as malicious men. They are loving and giving, focused and present. In 2000, I decided to attend New Mexico Military Institute, a military academy prep school, but after a semester I came to understand that the cliquish authoritarian nature of academy life was not for me. I left and went to college at a couple of community colleges in Illinois before deciding that I wanted to explore the world, meet people from many different life experiences, and exercise my passion to nurture and protect. Where could I find all three of those qualities and still sustain myself as a young woman in society? The military ... or so I thought.

I joined in June 2001 and left for Basic Training, which is the initial training phase that teaches military discipline, formations, and weapons training, in January 2002 at Fort Jackson. From Basic Training, I went to Advanced Individual Training (AIT), which teaches the job skill that the soldier was hired for, in March 2002 at Fort Huachuca. It was in these initial training stages that I began to understand that the foundations necessary for ensuring a safe and freer society anywhere were absent. Without at least a basic understanding and/or knowledge of others' history, language, customs, and sources of happiness, one could do nothing but act as a scared robot, waiting to be told what to do next when placed in a foreign environment.

At basic training I heard, and was instructed to sing, chants such as "Hi! Ho! Captin' Jack, meet me down by the railroad track, with that weapon in my hand, I'm gonna be a shootin' man, a killin' man..," "The bright red blood makes the green grass grow," etc. We did bayonet training, learned to use hand grenades, semi-automatic rifles, anti-personnel mines, rocket propelled grenade launchers, and many other weapons of mass destruction. Upon graduating from training, I was thoroughly disturbed by the lack of direction and foundational knowledge provided about the societies for which we had been trained to enter and impact. To ensure that these skills are not abused, but used in the most disciplined, reserved, and strategic fashion one must have an understanding of the people that they are interacting with. This was too much thought apparently because I was told upon requesting information about this component, "Specialist Cobb, where do you think you are?!" as the drill sergeant laughed at me.

Starting of a Conscientious Objection Process

After Basic Training and AIT ended, I spent about six months at an Army Reserve unit in Decatur, Illinois, before I began and finished reading a book called, In the Time of the Butterflies by Julia Alvarez. At the end of the book I had an epiphany. What I had signed up for does not match my spirit. To remain a part of an organization that forcibly occupies countries to secure business and power interests that can and will never create the peace that it markets as its motive, would be to self destruct into a long, slow and torturous death. I was visibly disturbed, so much so that a female sergeant at my unit came up to me at the next drill and asked me if I was OK. I told her what I was feeling and she said that I had to say something, and emphasized a sense of urgency about this task.

People at our unit had not yet begun to be mobilized, but mobilizations were beginning to be spoken of on the local news. I started writing the reasons for not being willing or able to participate anymore to support my request to be released from my military contract. At that point, I did not know that there was an official way to do everything in the military, including resist. As I wrote and printed out documents describing the conflict between my beliefs and the goal of the military, I later came to find that these were being discarded just as fast as they were coming in — and if not discarded, then disregarded by those officials that I presented them to.

In February 2003, I was told that I had to go to Wisconsin to go through the SRP (Soldier Readiness Process). I asked about the status of my case, in addition to inquiring about the purpose of going through the SRP in Wisconsin. I was assured that my case was being looked into and that all soldiers were going through SRP, just at varying times, not to worry. When I got there, it seemed as though I was in elementary school again, sitting at lunch tables in a gymnasium that reminded me of the one I attended while growing up. When we finally got past the hurry up and wait part, I found out why my intuition was sending off alarms when I received the call to go to Wisconsin. I was instructed that no Conscientious Objector case had been started, that I was no longer assigned to the unit in Illinois, and that I had one week to pack everything and move to Maryland. I was to join a Military Intelligence Batallion, which was waiting for its last few soldiers to trickle in before deploying — I was to be one of those last few soldiers.

One week? I didn't know where to start exactly, but I knew that I had to act. I withdrew from my classes at the local community college, I engaged the help of friends at The School for Designing a Society, and I prayed. I explained what was going on the best I could to my parents and friends, and I prayed. I packed all of the belongings that I thought I would want, while leaving behind things that might cause too much controversy or trouble, and I prayed.

Long story short, I arrived at Aberdeen Proving Ground on the night of March 3, 2003, and I handed in my official Conscientious Objector papers that morning. My friends at the School for Designing a Society assisted in gaining knowledge of the official conscientious objector process, and I made it known from the time I stepped foot onto that military post that I did not want any part of the military's business. I knew that in addition to the submission of official written opposition with supporting recommendations, I would have to undergo a chaplain's and a psychiatrist's interview, an informal hearing from an officer on base, and then wait for the Military Review Board to make its final decision. Once I arrived at the unit, I was immediately blessed in that my Commander assigned me to the Rear Detachment of the unit. He did not want me to deploy with the rest of the unit for fear that I would lower morale and be a threat to the unit's safety. I consider myself pretty nonviolent, but for the sake of my beliefs and the fact that I would have resisted deployment had I been ordered to, I had no complaints about being assigned to stay in the rear-detachment of the unit.

Effect of Military Life

As I spent more and more time on post, examples of deceit began to accumulate before my eyes, in addition to frustration and self-destructive behavior in troops due to not knowing why were being asked to deploy. I witnessed several people who had spent years in the military, as loyal believers and actors, were cut from the ranks a few years shy of their pension; military records, essential to proving eligibility for military-related disability claims, disappeared; a sergeant who had mistakenly been called onto active duty after his 20-year mark, was jailed and reduced to the lowest rank for becoming depressed and drinking in the barracks; even after the mistake had been identified and it was determined that he was to be released from service and awarded his retirement pension. Many frustrated, scared and confused young men and women had also taken to heavy drinking, and inflicting injuries upon themselves and others. In fact, I had never seen so many men cry in my life. It was in the military that I came to find that much like father, uncle, and I, up to the point of my change of consciousness, many of the men and women in the Armed Services had good intentions, it was the premise of these intentions that was often inaccurate or incomplete due to inaccuracies that have been indoctrinated in us from preschool on through our collegiate educations.

It was the military's disregard for honest and truthful consideration for those who were so loyal to them that alerted me to the fact that it was imperative that I seek sources to turn to should I need counsel. Shortly after my unit deployed to Iraq, my Commander began seeking to obtain the Full Bird Colonel rank, and in doing so, noticed that explaining my non-deployed status, as a fully able-bodied soldier, would be a problem for him. It was at this point that he threatened the use of legal consequences for disobeying a direct order; malingering, and conduct unbecoming of a soldier were tried against me, in an attempt to scare me into deploying. Thanks to the help of the *GI Rights Hotline*, the *Military Law Task Force*, and DC lawyer *Jim Klimaski*, I was able to deflect this threat as false, for my Commander had assigned me to the rear detachment himself and had signed an official contract with me to ensure that I would remain there until the end of my Conscientious Objector case.

While in Maryland at Aberdeen Proving Ground, I met a woman by the name of Claribel Torres a.k.a Claire or Jewelz, who became a dear friend of mine for that season of militarism in my life. She allowed me to stay at her home in Delaware, when we were allowed time away from the barracks, and in the barracks and on base, we stuck together very tight in sisterhood. When she deployed, I sent her care packages and we exchanged letters, and upon her return, I was even a bridesmaid in her second marriage. Although our friendship has since turned sour, she was very instrumental in my happiness while stationed at Aberdeen Proving Grounds. Many people in my unit, both enlisted and officers alike, openly shared similar beliefs about war and were supportive of my position, however, most were not willing to resist as did I, fearing the repercussions of doing so. The sexual assault that I experienced in the barracks, of which the legal resolution has still not been shared with me by the Criminal Investigation Division (CID) or the Judge Advocate General's (JAG) office of Aberdeen Proving Grounds, was one such matter that many in my unit were extremely supportive around.

Preventing another Person from being Swept under the Carpet

God, along with my friends and family, will always be steadfast pillars of support throughout my life. In addition, there were a whole host of men and women from the activist community that provided the brotherly and sisterly love that I required in order to make it through this experience. *Damu Smith, Jonah House, Joe Morton*, the *American Friends Service Committee, Not Your Soldier,* the *War Resisters League,* the *Anti-War, Anti-Racism Effort* (AWARE), *Not in Our Name, Anarchist People of Color, Suncere Ali Shakur,* the *Women of Color Resource Center,* the *Service Women's Action Network* (SWAN), *Alixa* and *Naima* of *Climbing Poetree,* and a wonderful group of student activists at Towson University (rest in peace Jordan) stood by my side throughout the process. It would be less than honest, to say that I felt that all were altruistically concerned with my interests. As a matter of fact, there was a point where I became disgusted with 90% of the activist groups that I came into contact with, for being treated as though I was a promotional opportunity rather than a human being. However in hindsight, I realize that all interest and invitations to participate in the various anti-war movement events were tools by which my case received the collective publicity necessary to prevent being another person swept under the carpet by the military bureaucracy. And for that I am grateful to all. To those that sincerely saw me as a person, in addition to the value of what my case represented, I love you and thank you.

Amy Goodman at *Democracy Now!*, *Eunice Buckner-Boone* at WEFT, *Ryme Khatkouda* at WPFW, *The Chicago Tribune*, and *The Guardian* provided the personal and media support that allowed me to survive the threats of being imprisoned for 2 years due to my beliefs. While I was misquoted in *The Chicago Tribune*, I am grateful to all for allowing resistance from within the military to be heard. Through these experiences, I learned the power of media, and the power of telling one's story.

In December 2003, my conscientious objector case was denied, as the final decision was rendered by the Military Review Board. I returned home to Illinois, where Chicago lawyer *Charles Nissam-Sabbat* assisted me in preparing and identifying a strategy to file a writ of habeus corpus appeal to uphold my position as a conscientious objector, despite the review board's decision, should I be mobilized and ordered to deploy again. After leaving the military, my dear friend *Cecil Smith, Jr.* was beautifully open and committed to helping me see/dream past my traumatic military experience and move forward in the spirit of my strengths. All in all and forevermore, my faith in God has allowed me to see my way past demons and on toward the blessings that lie within. I move forward in the light and harmony with which the world was created, and I give thanks to those who believe in and seek righteousness.

Anita Cole

In late November 2001, Anita Cole received her discharge from the U.S. Army as a conscientious objector to war.

"Before I entered the military, I felt as many people do. Generally speaking, I felt murder was wrong, but at times I considered killing unavoidable and even justified, such as in war. I am a person of intense conviction. My parents raised me believing that service to society — volunteering time and donating resources — is a moral imperative. Since I was a child, I have always been grateful that I am an American citizen and felt everyone should serve his or her country. The Armed Forces appealed to me as a meaningful, shared public effort. After graduating from college I decided to join the Army. I was not motivated to join the military for — nor did I receive — college loan repayment or any other monetary incentive. At the time of my enlistment, I felt full of pride and deeply fulfilled by my commitment to serve my country.

During Basic Training, bayonet training coupled with the mantra, "What makes the grass grow? Blood, blood, blood makes the grass grow", shocked me. But even at the time, I thought if I were called to war, then I would embrace the warrior spirit, too.

In August 2000, I was sent to the range to qualify on my assigned weapon, the M-16A2. I was deeply tormented and traumatized as I fired a deadly weapon at human silhouettes. Perceiving my obvious distress, one sergeant tried to offer me encouragement saying, "Come on, you're a killer!" At the time, I was so distraught that I was not able to qualify.

I told myself that I would only be, "poking holes in paper". This act of willful self-deception enabled me to qualify; however, the range NCO's words, "Come on, you're a killer", have continually haunted me. This comment cemented in my mind my objection to my duty as a soldier.

My conscience, ensuing meditation and reading, and introspection have compelled me to honor the true nature of my self. I will not be able to live in any sort of peace if I kill, let others kill, or support any act of killing in my thinking or in my way of life ... In other words, I am a conscientious objector in the literal sense."

This text has previously been published in The Broken Rifle No 70, May 2006. http://wri-irg.org/pubs/br70-en.htm

Tina Garnanez

"I was a lost Native", Tina Garnanez reflected on her journey in the Army. Tina grew up on a Navajo reservation and attended public school in Farmington, New Mexico. The only daughter of five children raised by a single mom, Tina enlisted when she was 17, to get money for college.

"I wanted to attend college, and I knew that between my family situation and being from the reservation, I had few options to get a college education."

Tina was stationed in Kosovo in March 2003 when US Planes started bombing Baghdad. In July 2004, Tina was deployed to Iraq. Tina had already completed her tour of duty, but the Army can extend a soldier's enlistment through a policy known as stop-loss. As a medic in Iraq, Tina transferred patients from the ambulances into the hospital where she saw the high cost of war. "I saw disfigured bodies, limbs blown off, soldiers who lost their sanity."

She also travelled with convoys delivering medical supplies to bases. On one of these convoys, Tina barely escaped an explosion. A bomb exploded and dust, rocks, shrapnel flew everywhere.

"I was so angry. Not angry at the Iraqis, but angry at the reason I was there. For what, I asked myself? My mom would have received a triangle-folded flag in exchange for her only daughter." She knew at the moment that she could no longer serve in this war. "I'm done", she said, "I am not fighting for anyone's oil agenda."

Tina is home in Silver City, New Mexico, honorably discharged. "I really wish I never went into the military. I now have Post Traumatic Stress Disorder. I jump at everything."

Tina says she speaks to a lot of high school students about why the recruiters target poor, minority students. These youth are looking for a way out, out of the ghetto, out of poverty, out of places where there is little hope for advancement. "The military is not the only option but it's usually only the military recruiters that are there in schools."

Tina has struggled to understand how she as a Native American could be part of the same machine that nearly exterminated the Native Americans. "Broken treaties. Forcing us on reservations. I was a lost Native." But Tina Garnanez has found her way as part of a growing movement of soldiers speaking out against the war in Iraq.

Tina Garnanez interviewed by Christine Ahn, Women of Color Resource Center, First published by War Times; Tiempo de Guerras. Reprinted in The Broken Rifle No 70, May 2006

Katherine Jashinski

I am a SPC in the Texas Army National Guard. I was born in Milwaukee, WI, and I am 22 years old. At age 19 I enlisted in the Guard as a cook because I wanted to experience military life. When I enlisted I believed that killing was immoral, but also that war was an inevitable part of life and, therefore, an exception to the rule.

After enlisting I began the slow transformation into adulthood. Like many teenagers who leave their home for the first time, I went through a period of growth and soul searching. I encountered many new people and ideas that broadly expanded my narrow experiences. After reading essays by Bertrand Russel and traveling to the South Pacific and talking to people from all over the world, my beliefs about humanity and its relation to war changed. I began to see a bigger picture of the world and I started to re-evaluate everything that I had been taught about war as a child. I developed the belief that taking human life was wrong and war was no exception. I was then able to clarify who I am and what it is that I stand for.

The thing that I revere most in this world is life, and I will never take another person's life. Just as others have faith in God, I have faith in humanity

I have a deeply held belief that people must solve all conflicts through peaceful diplomacy and without the use of violence. Violence only begets more violence.

Because I believe so strongly in non-violence, I cannot perform any role in the military. Any person doing any job in the Army contributes in some way to the planning, preparation or implementation of war.

For eighteen months, while my CO status was pending, I have honored my commitment to the Army and done everything that they asked of me.

Now I have come to the point where I am forced to choose between my legal obligation to the Army and my deepest moral values. I want to make it clear that I will not compromise my beliefs for any reason. I have a moral obligation not only to myself but to the world as a whole, and this is more important than any contract.

I will exercise my every legal right not to pick up a weapon, nor to participate in the war effort. I am determined to be discharged as a CO, and while undergoing the appeals process I will continue to follow orders that do not conflict with my conscience until my status has been resolved. I am prepared to accept the consequences of adhering to my beliefs.

Turkish Women Awaken to Conscientious Objection

By Ferda Ülker

L et us look at the current situation in Turkey before focusing upon the conscientious objector struggle and conscientious objector women.

Born to be Soldiers

The history of the Turkish Republic is the history of people who had come from an empire tradition and who later turned their faces to the West. All the reforms that followed the declaration of the Turkish Republic were targeting a bright future which would be more promising. The owners of this nation-(state)-building project were soldiers. However, this process beginning under the leadership of Ataturk in time has lost all its progressive qualities while the Turkish army has retained its unrivaled superiority. The recognition of the Turkish army's position as the saviour and defender of the political regime has almost gained a cultural character. The Turkish army has been regarded as an institution above of criticism, though its crushing effect has been felt on all the occasions it considered a threat to the regime, when it has undertaken frequent military coups which were *"powerful"* and *"destructive"*. The 12 September (1980) military coup has left heavy marks on all the Turkish people. These wounds are still waiting to be healed.

The basic thing we are taught in school is that we are an army-nation. As early as the first childhood years in school we swear to fight for this nation till the last drop of our blood. Every morning we promised to sacrifice ourselves as part of, and a gift to, the nation's existence.

"Every Turk is a soldier by birth" has been drilled into us. No matter what we do or who we are, we had no other choice than to be soldiers — by birth. We might not know what we want to do when we are grown up, but it was clear that we were soldiers and would stay so. Boys were little soldiers and we were little Ayses from the lyric of a children's song that goes like this:

> "Little soldier, little soldier tell me what you are doing?
> I am checking my gun, loading it with a bullet.
> Little Ayse little Ayse, tell me what you are doing?
> I am taking care of my baby. I am singing my baby a lullaby."

So, their future is set: Ayse to be a mother and the little soldier to be an adult soldier.

We are told that Turkey is surrounded by seas on three sides and surrounded by enemies on all four sides. The Turkish army produces enemies and threats and behaves in line with these scenarios to keep the Turkish people ready and aligned against all possible attacks. We, as Turkish people, are expected to have a military reflex. Any criticism of the army can result in an accusation of being a domestic enemy.

The history of the Turkish republic, during which all social life has been redesigned, has succeeded in injecting militarism into our daily lives as an indispensable part of our traditions. One of the direct results of this situation has been consideration of sexism as an almost natural and necessary part of social reality. Thus, militarism is an important element of sexism which stimulates and entrenches it.

Manhood and womanhood are described and codified in a way intrinsic to militarism, and any third possibility has been coded as sickness. The manhood of the Turkish army was saved when homosexuality was accepted as an incurable illness and homosexuals were exempted from military service on grounds of "disability".

In Turkey, women are not recruited in the army. This is, unfortunately, not a result of a long struggle or something accepted as good because military service is a bad thing. Women are regarded as the second sex, not appropriate for this sacred duty. Rather, women's place is considered to be at home, their duty taking care of children. The army is the place of real men and there is not a place for second or third sexes in the ranks. In this masculine world everything about women and womanhood is being used as an insult.

So in this case why are we, women who do not consider taking any position in the army whether invited or not, declaring ourselves as conscientious objectors and why do we say no to militarism?

Conscientious Objection in Turkey

In Turkey issues about the army are taboo and those taking up such issues are hurt badly. It would be unfair to neglect the role of the conscientious objector movement in the creation of today's environment in which we can, though in a limited way, talk and discuss about the army and militarism. The Conscientious objector movement has been maintained under very difficult conditions by very few people who give all their time and energy. Being in this movement, we have long been considered as interesting but weird even by the leftist opposition. We had a style and discourse very different from theirs and this made conception of the inner meaning of our word difficult for them. The Kurdish movement, too, chose to stay distant when they realised that the motto of *"neither army nor mountains (guerillas)"* is not a tactical but a basic principle for us.

Being a conscientious objector, walking with the conscientious objector movement, and advocating the right to conscientious objection in such a militarist environment, involves many risks of legal sanctions. Conscientious objection is not a concept defined by law in Turkey. For Turkish society, objection by men is just another name for cowardice in evading their duty. Objection by women is thought to be incomprehensible and sometimes unnecessary, not only for the society but also for leftist opposition movements, feminists and even some conscientious objectors. Because conscientious objection is considered to mean only rejection of military service duty, it is difficult to find a meaning in women's conscientious objection for many people and circles.

Conscientious objectors first appeared in the early 90s. A few years later, following the first objection declarations, *Izmir War Resisters Association* was founded. This association, consisting of a few activists who refused to see anti-militarism solely as a political line of thinking but also believing in the necessity of adopting it as a lifestyle, became the first meeting place for conscientious objectors. It has in a sense turned into "the centre" of any declaration of objection, any action or activity.

Conscientious objection has always been on the agenda on varying levels in different time periods. Even now there is no clarity on what sort of strategy is to be pursued. The struggle usually consists of reaction to the imprisonment of male conscientious objectors. Through the campaigns organised upon these imprisonments, we are trying to reach as many people as possible. However, it cannot be said that we truly qualify as a movement yet. The conscientious objector Working Group, which was formed inside the association, somehow failed in becoming functional. Till now, we still only come together to campaign when a conscientious objector faces an imprisonment threat.

Actions, activities and declarations are made within this framework. But, because of the heavy demands upon participants, only a few people end up able to go on. The campaign becomes weaker and dies. What are left are fatigue, with people hurt and distancing themselves. But there is a point not to be missed here: we are not the ones who determine the course of events. The imprisonment process is something that the military authorities control, perhaps this is an explanation why the campaigns fade away.

Personally, I don't believe that this not very brilliant picture is all that negative. Against all the odds, there is an ongoing process, and the possibility of evolution of this process into a much stronger movement in the future is always there. Even though we are few in number we haven't lost our hope. In Turkey, conscientious objection has been understood within an anti-militarism framework. Conscientious objection is an open area of struggle which takes its power from individuals and which is intrinsically antimilitarist. It is extremely important that the struggle rejects all militarism in all its components.

Women in the Conscientious Objector Struggle

Conscientious objection has been associated with men who declare themselves as conscientious objectors. The issue put by these conscientious objectors has been moulded and defined by them, most importantly by the compulsory military service duty. We women were seeing ourselves not as the agents but supporters of the struggle. As we got involved, we have started to see the crucial importance of inclusion of women in the conscientious objector struggle. On the other hand, we still could not show the courage to say "yes, here we are in the struggle" for a long time. One of the reasons for this can be the militarist culture which had its effect on us. Having been raised in this cultural environment, even when we participate in oppositional movements, we may fail to get rid of the marks of it. We get fearful as women even when we are a part of oppositional movement gatherings. When we come up with an idea and need to express it, we wait to make our point fully, clearly enough not to leave room for debate. But time passes by while we wait.

We failed to argue that conscientious objection is not an area limited and peculiar to men, that if accepted as such this might lead us into sexism, and that conscientious objection, though it relates to army and military duty, still necessitates a broader perspective. It has taken a considerable amount of time for women to pluck up courage and come out with their views. On 15 May 2004, in the first Militourism Festivity gathering, our five friends declared their conscientious objection. Their courage, despite the criticisms implying "OK what is it to do with you?", encouraged us to declare our conscientious objection later on. Currently there are 62 conscientious objectors in Turkey and 13 of them are women. These numbers may seem small but when the short history of this struggle and the effect of militarist culture are taken into account, it is not to be underestimated.

What happened to make women pluck up their courage to come out? In my opinion the main reason for this was that we reached a point where we had to decide to be counted. What we were fighting for was more than to be associated solely with demanding exemptions from military service for conscientious objector men. It would be possible to broaden the agenda of conscientious objection only through the appearance of women in the struggle, and questions being asked. Yet we were expecting a difficult process and we were waiting for a suitable time. For me the right time would come when some pioneering women appeared and come out before me. For the five friends of us, on the other hand, the right time was the National Tourism Festivity preparations which had taken a great deal of time and which had excited all of us. That all five women had decided to acknowledge their objection together can be accounted for by their being encouraged by being together. We knew that there would be many "why" questions, but we had raised and matured our answers to such questions during the past years and the time had come.

Declarations by Women Conscientious Objectors

These short quotations from the declarations of the conscientious objector women make the point better than I can, since they express our approach clearly.

Inci Aglagul, the first woman conscientious objector:
"I will consider myself complicit as long as I stay silent. But by no means do I want any complicity with war and militarism, or to watch passively the imprisonment of our lives, our minds and our dreams. I will not take part in any mechanism undermining the living. Because of these views, I refuse military service, militarism, and this compulsion as a lifestyle."

Nazan Askeran (recently deceased):
"I refuse any type of violence regardless of its being organised/unorganised. I don't want to die or kill in wars. I object to being a threat too, a terminator of the living/inorganic life that will exist on this planet after us. I refuse the militarist approach which introduces and legitimises it to oppress, to be oppressed; to give orders, to take orders; to die, to kill; the war, the military service, the violence in all fields of our lives."

Let's listen to the voice of Ceylan Ozerengin:
"Let all live and act as they want and think right. In my opinion, human life is the only sacred concept on the earth. I reject all the other 'holy duties' forced upon us, totally."

Ayse Girgin:
"As a woman, although I don't relate to militarism through the army, I face up to it in every field of my life. I struggle against militarism as much as possible, in this world involving all sorts of relations based on hegemony-oppression, sexist discrimination and any type of violence, bloody or non-bloody. I refuse all faces of militarism."

Figen:
"... Even though they are not drafted, women are the most oppressed group under militarism. As a patriarchal ideology, militarism defines our whole lives and causes women to be perceived in the society as property, servants, slaves, objects to be silenced and harassed/raped. In Turkey, with traces of the military coup, military rule and an ongoing war, women's liberation is possible through the struggle against militarism.

I declare my objection in the name of millions of children whose lives were divided into two after the military coup of the September 12 of 1980. We witnessed and lived the terror during and after the 12th of September.

People we loved got killed, got lost, sent into exile or made so frightened that we learned what fear is very well. We figured out what armies are for on the September 12 coup. The army is fear, the army exists to give fear. The army is terror..."

The common point in the women's declarations is that their views are based on a critique of militarism from a feminist point of view. The main point is the making clear and the refusal of militarism, regardless of the form in which it manifests itself. Traditionally, the relation of women to military service is thought to be within the context of their being mothers, sisters, wives, girlfriends of would-be-soldiers. However, women conscientious objectors, most of them being feminist and antimilitarist, talk in their declarations about ways of relating to the army other than those mentioned above.

Men try to explain women's role in the conscientious objector movement as her being a wife, sister or mother of a male conscientious objector. This view has been accepted. If no such connection exists, men say, maybe the woman has a close friend among male conscientious objectors. But obviously all these reasons for women's involvement in the conscientious objection movement assume a men-bounded existence for women. Our declarations elaborate why we are here, inside. Of course we are supporting the stand of male conscientious objectors refusing to comply with compulsory military service, as everybody else sensitive to the issue does. But what we do primarily is to make visible the militarism which penetrates all sectors of social life, all social relations. We want it to be clearly seen, so that we will be able to fight against it.

Doubtlessly, those types of relations called "traditional" of themselves are also objectionable, but when we consider the existing profile, in our declarations, these contexts are appropriated. Women conscientious objectors construct their relation to militarism through their own existence and own "problems", rather than through "men" in their lives. As clearly put in our declarations, we do not consider conscientious objection as just a rejection of "obligatory military service", but instead as a confrontation with militarism.

What Do Women's and Men's Objections Mean?

The common point in the declarations of women and men objectors is their antimilitarist standing and the harsh criticism directed against militarism without hesitation. The target is to detect and display militarism in every sense of the term and within all contexts and to declare that in no way will the objectors engage with militarism. No conscientious objector declaration, without regard to whether men's or women's, limits itself to demanding just the abolition of compulsory military service. Rather, they are geared to the aim of revealing militarism as a vicious, criminal practice and a declaration that this crime will never be condoned.

107

At this point, a different process is put into motion which results in differentiation of the objections of men and women conscientious objectors. Men may face forced recruitment and imprisonment. This risk imposes on men conscientious objectors their accepting a "civil death".

For women, such a risk of detention or imprisonment has not yet arisen. But this does not mean that such a thing will never happen. Presently, usually neither men nor women face prosecution. However, some men are prosecuted and punished for not complying with orders. For women, the only judicial risk stems from the article criminalising "deterring public from fulfilling their military service duty". Until now no woman has been prosecuted in this way. I believe this partly stems from not being taken seriously.

The military has many tools to counteract men's conscientious objector declarations. As a movement, we try to get into a process which is already determined by others. When it comes to women conscientious objectors, the military does not seem to have a policy. Women's conscientious objection has a potential which shows that the militarist culture of society is not inevitable or eternal. The key to save the conscientious objection struggle from the fires of criticisms — seeing men's conscientious objection as cowardice or treason — is the declarations of woman conscientious objectors. Women's involvement in the conscientious objector movement promises to carry the movement to another stage. In this sense it is desirable to see an increase in the number of the questions "why" and "what are you trying to say". The answers to these questions may open the door of a new world. Maybe it is too soon to say such a thing, but when I imagine street demonstration of thousands of woman conscientious objectors I can also dream of a chance to reach people's consciousness, getting through the dust and corruption of the ages. But for such a fantastic dream to become true there are tasks for all of us. The first and foremost is to undertake the responsibility of fulfilling the requirements of being a movement.

Needs of Women Conscientious Objectors

Despite all the criticisms against being a woman conscientious objector, we are here as women conscientious objectors and will keep on existing. Being in this struggle for three years, our first need is to get to know each other better and create a common language explaining our political stance. I do not know what the needs are for women conscientious objectors in the world, but what we need first here is to work out this common ground. We still have a short history.

As woman conscientious objectors living in Turkey, our most urgent need is to ascertain the points where we have shared and differed in views and to create a language which reflects the widest consensus possible among us. We all share the criticism of militarism in our declarations but the arguments behind these criticisms differ.

However, a point constantly overlooked is that we are a component of the antimilitarist struggle. And certainly we are aware of the wide spectrum of antimilitarism. When we look at the relation of conscientious objection to women, apparently we are still at the very beginning of the road. In fact it is an important opportunity for the antimilitarist struggle that we are in the position of reinforcing these questions. Because the stronger the questions are, the more solid the answers will be. In this context, it is a fact that international communication and sharing of experiences will contribute to us both morally and practically.

Thanks to Alp, Ash, Cuneyt and Ulku for help with translation and editing.

I REJECT

Ferda Ülker

Since I have defined myself as an anti-militarist and a feminist, naturally I believe I am an objector. By means of this declaration, I turn this "informal" situation into a "formal" situation!

The conscientious objection movement is not only a struggle against "compulsory conscription". This expression includes a wider dimension. And we, women, have a bigger voice and status, than being only a "supporter" of the movement. Conscientious objection is direct opposition to militarism and every aspect of it. Militarist thought does not only remain within the border of the military, but it envisions a military world that affects daily life. And in this world, women are degraded and disregarded. Their status is always secondary, even though occasionally circumstances require a woman to advance her position. Its terms are: authority, hierarchy, and obedience.

These expressions are very familiar and significant to us, women.

These are the well-known barriers of a world that continuously pushes us back. Militarism is always like a unannounced and shameless guest in every aspect of life, especially for women living in this region; in the streets, at home, at work, in our relationships, in our fields of struggle, and everywhere.

I declare that, today, as much as before, I shall defy every secret and obvious form of militarism and show solidarity with anyone who defies militarism.

As much as militarism is determined to affect my life, I am determined to continue my struggle.

I REJECT!

A Feminist Perspective on Conscientious Objection in Turkey

By Hilal Demir, War Resisters' International

Why did we, Turkish women, declare conscientious objection though we are not subject to compulsory military service in Turkey? Here I record some problems and dynamics of conscientious objection, the contributions of women's conscientious objection declarations to the movement, and the resulting discussions.

Living in a patriarchal culture, I think that all the opposition movements, including feminism, have the continuous risk of becoming *"masculinized"*. This is a risk so strong as to cause the fading away of most movements.

In my opinion, when the feminist perspective is overlooked in a movement against patriarchy and its practices, the process will fail. In a movement like antimilitarism, anti-sexism should be regarded as one of the most fundamental elements of the struggle against militarism. For, leaving this *"attention"* out of account, insidious mechanisms of the patriarchal system will not only leak into the movement but will also trivialise it. I would like to quote from an essay by Pınar Selek for the feminist theoretical magazine Amargi:

> While this is a very important issue with regards to militarisation and the reproduction of masculinity, it remains as one agenda item among many in the struggle that needs to be waged against militarism. Especially here in Turkey we have an abundance of militarism issues to be dealt with. There is a need to settle accounts with history, with the republic, with the dominant approach, even with the opposition itself. There is a need to develop politics against the militarization of policies and the economy, against the rapid institutionalization of militarism. But from the outset, the anti-militarist movement has failed to go beyond the issues of "compulsory military service" and "alienation from military service". The contribution of the feminist movement will save the anti-militarist movement from this agenda and the patriarchal attitude it is stuck with. To the extent that they fail to produce a feminist agenda and public debate against militarism, nationalism and politics that organise war through integration with micro powers, anti-war and anti-militarist attempts will always go back to square one. In order to prevent going back to square one, the anti-militarist movement needs to integrate with the feminist movement. It always has. [1]

As women who have participated actively in antimilitarist, antiwar and conscientious objection movements, we have been looking for alternative ways to express our resistance to militarism. We have struggled to find a space for ourself in existing movements due to the lack of a gender perspective in those movements. In 1999 we were a group of activist women working in the *Izmir War Resisters' Association* who formed the independent women's group *"Antimilitarist Feminists"*. This group was the first to establish itself in order to overcome the problems women were facing in the movements due to the simple fact that they were women. Similar groups have been formed in various cities in the following years.

In Turkey, as in most other places in the world, it is common to define conscientious objection as objection to performing compulsory military service. Since women do not have to perform military service, their declaration of conscientious objection is considered a deviation. My prime motivation in declaring my objection was calling attention to the risk of this movement becoming some kind of forum for male politics and reminding us that militarism can't be confined to military service. That women have no *"place"* in the Turkish army is due to the perception that we are not deemed worthy of such a *"noble"* institution. This means that compulsory service is not just a practice of *"national defence"*, but also serves to differentiate between men's and women's citizenship and their place in society.

When I was thinking about what to write in my declaration, the points which I wanted to explore in the text were very obvious for me. Reasons for wars, how people are used in wars, how daily militarism prepares us mentally for wars and for violence, how the structured social life with gender roles makes their system long-lived. So in my declaration I simply reject all of these points. One of the women who did research on women's conscientious objection in Turkey is *Esra Gedik*. Some of her evaluation of our situation follows.

Women who declare their objection though they are not recruited, do it as a confrontation against militarism, against all forms of war, violence and discrimination. Besides, the addressees of this attitude are the armed forces and war itself. It is the war economy and war mentality. The most oppressed by militarism are women, as militarism is meshed with sexism, patriarchy, heterosexism and all kinds of discrimination. For that reason, women's confrontation is significant. It is the rejection of the armies, of all the wars caused and led by them, of armaments and all kinds of arms and violence as a whole, by a woman as a mother, a peace advocate, an antimilitarist and a human. And it is the evidence of women having more to say and do in this movement in spite of being *"supporters"*. Although women are not recruited, they are sometimes part and generally victims of this phenomenon. They therefore raise their voice against all kinds of authoritarian, hierarchical, nationalist, sexist and militarist structures as they don't want to die or kill or be oppressed and exploited. Remaining silent would be supporting war. There is a will for a world without armaments, racial, religious or sexist discrimination [2].

I made my declaration on 15 May 2004 during the *"mili-tourism festival"* we had organised. With the emphasis we have in our declarations, we run the same risk as male objectors of being tried under the same legislation. This is a political strategy to try to force the government of the Turkish Republic to adopt a definite position on conscientious objection. Women's conscientious objection declarations contribute to this strategy. A common point of the women's declarations is a feminist attitude towards militarism. Most definitions of conscientious objection include the human right to freedom of conscience and conscientious objection as a personal expression of this conscience. As a feminist I don't think it problematic to declare myself as a conscientious objector.

The first legal case for the conscientious objection movement in Turkey was that of Osman Murat Ülke in 1996. There were many problems in relation to this man's case, due to the length of the process, uncertainties, burn-outs, material insufficiencies, lack of activism, marginalisation, and lack of support from other political movements. This led to exhaustion, and created problems that would continue to haunt the conscientious objection movement in the years that followed. The impact of the culture we live in, continuing exhaustion, and deficiencies led the movement to limit itself to conscientious objection declarations made by men who refuse to serve in the army. Consequently, *"hero worship"* was inevitable, since the men were running a risk of long prison terms in a country without any legal provision for conscientious objection in the constitution.

Refusal of military service by men and their subsequent elevation to *"heroism"* status may accelerate the movement to some degree, but subsequent strategies should aim to devalue this *"heroism"*. Otherwise the movement would become a men-only movement. In fact, the conscientious objection movement has gained such characteristics lately. *"Heroism"* is both a male and a militarist concept we should criticise. It is obvious that we need to develop new strategies and attitudes. The only action we have thought of so far is conscientious objection activism, and we women have our share of the responsibility here. We fail to make priorities that give us the time to raise the points that we find important. I don't intend to be too harsh in my criticism, but I think that what we have neglected most of all is the subject of the problems we face as women.

Recently we have started to discuss an important question: *"Although we are sure that we want to implement antimilitarist and feminist perspectives and action as women on any problem, is the conscientious objection platform the right place for it?"* The background for this question is that we use the concept of *"women objector"* in a way that most people, including women in the conscientious objection movement and anti-militarist movement, do not. They think that the term *"objection"* was created for a legal situation, and that it should be restricted to this use. They are against the declaration of women's conscientious objection. They argue that women can create changes on their own terms developed by them. Since we as women have our own power, we can create our own words against militarism, rather than change the *"conscientious objection"* term.

I think that the conscientious objection declarations of 12 women have led to greater gender sensitivity within the movement. The declarations have challenged the discussions on this concept and encouraged us to search for a path for new perspectives. Women's objection declarations keep us awake, help us grow stronger, and prevent our movement from being focused only on men being judged.

The one and only activism practice I can see within the antimilitarist movement is conscientious objection. And if women who are made invisible by militarism are also ignored in their activism we will be trapped in the very militarist pitfall itself. But there are still important questions to consider: should women's efforts to become visible be made in the field of conscientious objection in order to become *"equalised"* with men? And how should anti-sexist attitudes be encouraged within the movement? On the other hand, women's declarations have brought up the following questions mentioned by *Ayşegül Altınay* in Amargi:

- Who and which processes give birth to *"Soldier Turks"* (and their *"militant"* counterparts)? How come we believe we are *"born"* soldiers as a society and think that the most meaningful contribution to the society is military service?
- Where do men and women stand in the *"soldier-nation"* thesis?
- If we take militarism in its broadest definition as glorification of military assets and practices and *"civil"* life becoming shaped by them, what is our contribution to militarism as *"civil"* people?
- What is the contribution of women?
- What is the contribution of us, feminists? Can we sustain our declarations and practice against all kinds of violence and militarism?
- To summarise, when will we truly confront the processes of *"being"* and *"making"* soldiers and militarism? If we are not born soldiers what can we do to resist becoming soldiers? [3]

Recently we had a gathering with women from different cities to engage in these discussions. We continue to discuss conscientious objection and are preparing strategies for new extensions. Our common needs led us to establish a women's network. We have started discussing various conceptions and ways of developing antimilitarist women's activism. And I see that we begin to have results in the process which began in practice with women objectors.

Thanks to Balam Kenter for translating the quotes from Turkish to English.

Footnotes

[1] Pınar Selek, *"Feminizme ve anti-militarizme ihtiyacımız var* (We need feminism and anti-militarism" Amargi, S.2, Autumn Issue 2006, p27.

[2] Esra Gedik, *"Kadınlık ve Vicdani Red Üzerine"* (About Femininity and Conscientious Objection) Amargi, S.2, Autumn Issue 2006, p38.

[3] Ayşe Gül Altınay *"'Asker Türk'leri Ve Onların Asker Kardeşlerini Kim Doğuruyor?"* (Who is giving birth to "Soldier Turks" and their soldier brothers?) Amargi, S.2, Autumn Issue 2006, p18.

Conscientious Objection Declaration

I don't want to live in a world which is sexist, hierarchical, authoritarian, militarist and patriarchal.

I do not want them to give me their system-based school education ...

I do not want people to die in wars for the sake of a huge deception.

I do not want to have to prove myself as a fully intelligent being and individual because of being a woman.

I do not want to brush aside the state's war policies and their lies.

I do not want militaries who train up dummies to die in wars ...

I do not want people to decide anything for me without asking me ...

I do not want to see militarist concepts and behaviours within our movements ...

I do not want to live under patriarchal rules, and behaviours which invade my private life.

I do not want somebody to judge people's sexual identities.

I do not want to be ruled by labels such as "mother", "wife", "daughter" and "girlfriend" just because I am a woman ...

I do not want to live fenced in by borders ...

I do not want to kill and be killed ...

And ... I am rejecting all of these by listening to my conscience ...

Because I WANT to live free and happy in a world where there is no war, nor any kind of violence, and which is anti-authoritarian, without borders.

And you?

Hilal Demir

This statement was first published in Izmir, Turkey in 2005

Women Activists in South Korea's Peace Movement

By Jungmin Choi, Solidarity for Peace and Human Rights

Militaristic Landscapes after Democratisation

Militarism in South Korea is based on the military, and the conscription system has considerable influence not only on men's life, but also on women's. Its influence ranges widely from direct and physical violence to the cultural and emotional atmosphere of society. Various difficulties face women activists in the field of conscientious objection to military service, national security, and peace and disarmament. This reveals the deep-rooted militarism in the South Korean society. Here I have put my impression and experiences as an activist who is interested in pacifism and feminism.

Korea, as the only divided country in the world, is a place where military tension and possibility of armed conflicts between North and South exist. Although the distance between North and South has been mitigated throughout the long process of the reunification movement and neo-liberalist globalisation, society's belief in militaristic security still continues. Throughout history, Koreans have viewed military and national defence as concepts that are fundamental to the national existence. This anxiety about security — especially in terms of the military system — has allowed the *"Don't Ask"* conscription system to continue, and further, made people believe that the violation of human rights within the military is inevitable to a certain extent.

As the traditional notion of *"security"* is emphasised, the sex difference becomes more specific, and masculine belligerence and violence are celebrated. This behaviour pattern is generally shown in international relations, the cold war, weapons competition, and relationships between women and men. Not to our surprise, the military is portrayed as an active defender of peace. In Korea, where the conscription system has been heavily enforced, it is undeniable that the images of women as protected, weak and second-class citizens have been required to form and maintain the power of militaristic culture and even the military itself. In Korean society where the balance of power is understood as the only way of survival, only men whose bodies are fit for combat and their masculinity are valued. Consequently, women, and people with disabilities who do not have such bodies, become marginalised. For this reason, the conscientious objectors in Korea are often compared to the emasculated or women; they become the second-class citizens who are excluded from society.

The army and national defence has a deeply complicated history and ideology in South Korea. During more than 30 years of dictatorship, the military has become a sanctuary beyond the constraints of civil monitoring. There have been numerous violations of human rights inside the army, which continue to this day. Even as South Korea in general has developed in a more democratic direction, these transformations do not apply to military-related matters, as if the military is an exception from democracy. It is an open secret that the privileged few abuse their power to exempt their sons from military service. South Korea does not have universal conscription, since it is only men without money or power who are drafted.

Recently, nationalism and patriotism in Korea — which serve as the foundation of self-reliant national defence — have been quite threatening. Not only the conservatives but also the leftists long for a country that would not have to take notice of other powerful countries, that would maintain its policy without regard to superpowers, and exercise its sovereign authority. Of course this kind of patriotism interplays with the military. It is now common to see popular young male celebrities proudly advertise their enlistment, promote patriotism, and witch-hunt those who evaded military service. Unlike in the past where the majority of people viewed going into the military as the *"end of a celebrity's career"*, performing military service in order to protect women and family now improves their popularity. In contrast, one pop-star who was able to legally escape conscription due to his US citizenship is not allowed to return to Korea simply because he changed his earlier statement that he would give up US citizenship and go to the military.

Women and the Military

The debates around a court decision to rule preferential treatment (granting extra points for the men with active military service experience in search of a job) as unconstitutional clearly shows how women's lives — often perceived to be unrelated to the military — are actually related to the military or conscription system in one way or another. On 23 December 1999, when the Constitutional Court declared the bonus point policy unconstitutional because it violates national equality, men who were provoked by the court's decision committed cyber terrorism on the websites of women's organisations and Ewha Woman's University, the school the litigant went to. The websites were covered with swear words and threats and the activists at women's organisations suffered from vomiting and headaches. In the end, the website had to be shut down. Afterwards, such acts have become popular, and consequently, feminist websites that criticised military or militaristic culture have all been devastated or shut down by men's terrorist actions. In some cases, the profile of the writer or owner of the website was disclosed to internet pornography sites. For example, one woman suffered from over 60 phone sex calls a day. The suffering at Ewha Woman's University did not stop there. In 2003 in the midst of the social debate over conscientious objection, Ewha's homepage was once again shut down because the student government supported the conscientious objection movement.

Since then, the Ewha's website became known as the headquarters of the feminist movement, constantly being attacked by the militarist men whenever there is a social debate on women and military.

The position of the *"strong protector"* is only maintained by the gratitude and respect of the protected (for example, the practice of writing a thank-you letter to random soldiers, which used to be done in elementary school). Those who are second-class citizens, including women who do not serve in the military or people with disabilities, who are only to be protected, are not supposed to voice their opinions.

One of the common questions that I get as a conscientious objection movement activist is *"why do women who don't even serve in the military discuss the issue of military?"*. This question shows the ideology of Korean society that has silenced women's voices on the military or conscription, both visibly and invisibly.

In my early days in the movement, I was able to argue about the issues online because I was perceived as a male due to my gender-neutral name. When I talk to someone whom I have not met yet in person, the person is always surprised that I am a woman. Now I am used to people's surprised reply *"you are a woman?"*. In contrast, for TV debates or newspaper stories that need a photo, I did not have many opportunities to show my face. Not only because the host cared about the fact that I am a woman, but also because I was concerned for myself considering what had happened to the women speakers in previous instances. My self-censorship was so increased by these experiences that I found myself speaking about military, conscription, or issues on militarism only to a limited extent, or looking for a male writer even when one was not requested. My colleagues in the movement who experienced cyber terrorism against the student government of Ewha Woman's University say that, to this day, they still do not tell strangers that they are its alumnae. People believe that women are not able to discuss anything related to military issues. This kind of experience-based responses — that women who do not serve in the military lack the authority to speak — defines the military as an exclusively masculine/male domain, restricting women's access to it. This attitude prevents people from seeing how the Korean military and the Korean militaristic culture have been intensifying the mechanism of gender roles, the exploitation of human rights, and of a woman's right to live. For these reasons, Korean women are perceived as speaking out against the abrogation of the bonus point system, and conscientious objection, in the context of being positioned as the wife or the mother of a soldier.

The Beginning of the Conscientious Objection Movement

For almost 60 years, people have continuously objected to military service, and been punished for their objection. But they never became a matter of interest until a weekly news magazine ran the issue as the cover story in early 2001. Before this article on the conscientious objection of *Jehovah's Witnesses*, this society had treated conscientious objectors as if they were invisible. Not once before having a proper social discussion, it is now becoming a controversial issue.

When we formed the conscientious objector movement, we started from showing the suffering of conscientious objectors and their families. Actually there were many people who were viciously beaten, sometimes even to death, for not holding a gun under the military dictatorship. The most urgent necessity was to regain the impaired reputation of conscientious objectors, and not with 100 logical words but to evoke an emotional echo to the society. According to our expectations, it caused a great stir in society, with people fully realising how excessive the governments violation was and how irresponsible it was for all of us to neglect it. But then we ran into systematic flak from the Ministry of National Defence and conservative Christian groups. They slyly represented conscientious objectors as equivalent to the privileged few who illegally dodge the draft. Also they placed excessive emphasis on the fact that most conscientious objectors believe in a specific religion so that it could be a special treatment for heretics. Soon, society turned its back on conscientious objectors, and no more rational discussion was possible.

Conscientious Objection Movement and Women

In almost every movement, feminist critique on male-dominated activism is not a new story any more. Feminist criticism, which took place in different forms in different fields, often faced strong opposition. To my understanding, the foundation for such an argument is that, feminist critique undermines the greater cause of the movement or erases the possibility of other more effective ways of resistance. However, I believe that the feminist challenge in both peace movements and women's movements is not a mere attempt to create problems. Rather, it originates from ultimate differences in perspectives on peace. Women refused to be viewed as a singular group and to generalise our differences, and questioned where we stood within that name, *"women"* or *"we"* in reality. Moreover, women resisted the ways in which our sufferings get objectified for the purpose of the anti-US movement or of class struggle. We asked people to rethink and redefine the activist methodology that reproduces male-dominated behaviour.

Women's marginalisation within the conscientious objection movement has to do with the short seven-year history of the movement. Fighting the resistance to and violence against the movement, we had no choice but to compromise our argument. This strategy has its positive sides; it shows the suffering and pain of the objector and people around him including family and friends. Nevertheless, it is also true that such representation also distorts the objectors' suffering to meet the social expectation of them. Here, an objector is viewed as a *"pitiful"* victim of the state's violence rather than an active resister to militarism. Consequently, the conscientious objectors — regardless of their real character — had to become *"good people"* who silently endured social criticism. This not only put a burden on themselves but also contributed to their supporters' marginalisation — especially the women. This phenomenon was more common in the alternative social-service movement where the activism was excessively focused on the individual objectors where women only became secondary role players as supporters (for example, providing assistance to those in jail). On the other hand, in order to criticise the strong masculinity that society expects for men, the individual objectors themselves had to be super-heroes. They had no choice but to object to military service, not because they are extraordinarily brave but because they are weak — too weak to even be trained for military service that could possibly hurt someone. These gendered roles expected for women activists as well as the atmosphere that stresses blind obedience frustrated women activists and obscured what our movement aimed for.

Personally I hope that the conscientious objection movement becomes a movement that provides an opportunity for us to see where we are located in this society where violence is normalised, and whether we are a part of such violence. I hope it will be a movement that pushes us to think how violence gets created in our society and to make sure that we do not allow it to become a part of our daily lives — rather than understanding the world and setting the role of the movement through the public sphere and grand discourse.

Thinking of the conscientious objection movement as a process rather than a result: Wouldn't this be true peace activism?

Thanks to Dongyoung Kim for translation from Korean to English

Paraguayans Unite Against Militarism

By María Elena Meza Barboza, Movimiento de Objeción de Conciencia Paraguay

I n Paraguay, the poorest sectors of society are criminalised through the state machine, its military, police and even judicial structures, which pave the way for repressing or depriving people of their access to basic facilities, such as sanitation, education and housing.

Militarism in Paraguay

In Paraguay, the military is still very strong in terms of its structure, in the sense that there are many cartels or military detachments. Furthermore, a greater budget is allocated to the military than to health and education. This diversion of economic and human resources to the military is harmful to the population because of the army's repression of the people, especially affecting the poorest sectors of society.

Despite the State, with its military and police structures, having improved in many aspects regarding democracy, there is still a long way to go. This is because this institution does not protect its people. We also have problems relating to judicial power: it only exists for the powerful and those who have money.

Recently, the military has had too much time and money on their hands. First they created the conflict with Bolivia [1]. Then they started repressing, or generating fear amongst, the people. They would be outside schools with their weapons and uniform so that nobody would misbehave, because the schoolchildren would protest — including breaking down doors — if the authorities tried to confront them.

From then on they were all over the capital — they were in schools, in shopping centres, in squares, on street corners, everywhere; at one point it seemed like we were in a state of siege.

Then it seemed that the number of soldiers on the streets had decreased, perhaps due to the different actions which we carried out as MOC (*Movimiento de Objeción de Conciencia* — Conscientious Objection Movement), and also due to the pressure of society in general. Then, however, the state created an urban guard in Asunción which was only for the city centre. At that point this urban force was expanding slowly so as not to draw attention to themselves and they were skirting round El Banado, which is the area where the poor live (well, according to the army, they are criminals).

Within the country, they also had the idea of invading the territories of the campesino (rural farmers) and indigenous settlements [2], in addition to the continued coercions and the fact that the campesino protests resulted in deaths.

The Antimilitarist Movement in Paraguay

From the very beginning, MOC was the only antimilitarist movement which continued to oppose the armed forces and the violent culture of our country. Although this is a country which preserves military culture, such as patriarchy, machismo, submission and violent conflict resolution, our movement has been struggling against these values since the beginning. It has not been easy, but now we can say we have made great progress with satisfactory achievements. Above all, we are visible in society: one of these achievements is having established the right to conscientious objection and there continue to be people who declare themselves as objectors, not only in Asunción but throughout the entire country.

The declaration of objectors has been possible because we broke with the fear concerning the right of objection. This fear still existed even once the right to object had been enshrined in the National Constitution.

In 1995 the first female conscientious objector publicly declared herself as such [3]. Since then, women of MOC have declared themselves as objectors on a daily basis. Another group of women declared themselves as objectors in 2002 [4], includeding some famous women. Another group of women of MOC and from society in general publicly declared themselves in 2004, but the Congress did not want to issue conscientious objector cards to the women because the Constitution does not impose compulsory military service for women.

Furthermore, the way in which we resolve conflicts and the nonviolent actions which we carry out are being considered as alternatives which people are using and including in their groups. Very often, other movements call us to ask for training as to what NVDA (NonViolent Direct Action) is, and they ask us to be their security force in their demonstrations. This shows that people prefer our approach, which provides nonviolent solutions to conflicts.

We are allies of many social movements, as well as student movements from Banados, children and teenager's movements, health, victims of Ycuá Bolaños (a big supermarket that burned down on 1 August 2004, leaving almost 400 dead and more than 500 injured), etc. And this gives us the strength to do things everyday, because this means social recognition. It means that what we are doing is worth it even if we are a small movement. Despite there being only about 10 of us, we are very happy doing what we are doing.

Being a Conscientious Objector

In MOC, there is only one organisation, both for men and women. There are no differences and there is no separate feminist anitimilitarist movement. There is only one organisation for women antimilitarists and our activities are based on the significance of antimilitarism, conscientious objection and a culture of peace. This is what MOC is about. We appreciate the support of our fellow male colleagues and this is not a problem for the women working in MOC.

Regarding military service, it is obligatory for men, and even children are conscripted, and this happens above all in the heart of the country. The declaration of women objectors is not recognised by the state because the law on military service does not include women, and therefore women are not given permission to object. Despite this, in some cases we do achieve our goals. It all depends on the current situation and the pressure which we exert. In any case, despite these obstacles, there are many women objectors.

People in society often ask why there are women in the movement if the military service is not obligatory for them. People think that objection only affects men. Fortunately, we have shown on more than one occasion that this is not the case and that militarism affects all of us, that violence affects us all. Within the movement, there is no opposition to women objectors.

Many people think that MOC is a movement which is made up of men only, but MOC, since the beginning, was a group made up of both men and women where everyone has the same influence in the decision-making process, as these decisions are made based on consensus. At some point in the movement's history, there were more women than men within the movement. This is seen in a positive rather than a negative light, as it gives the movement more strengh and legitimacy. Furthermore, people ask us women why we are part of MOC given that the military service does not affect us. We always reply that it does affect us. It affects all of us; women, children and adults in general, because we all want a better life. Every individual who is part of this society contributes to this society we live in, be it in the taxes we pay, in the social movements we join, fighting for a certain ideology, through our jobs — simply not doing anything can also be counted as being complicit with the military system. Therefore, the MOC women decided to be antimilitarist because every day we are working together so as to change this machista culture which exists in Paraguayan society and which affects us so much. We want to end the domination of the powerful classes over the poor, over children, over indigenous populations and also over us women. Therefore we are doing our part every single day.

We do not like the offer which the armed forces and the State have made to their citizens. They say, *"We are giving women a sphere of influence. See, we are not machista anymore, we are no longer discriminating against women as they too can serve in the military."* But we ask what purpose this serves, as they are merely going to learn the same concepts which have always been taught in the armed forces: to kill, torture, oppress the people, and be complicit in injustices carried out by the government in power at the time.

So, in relation to the incorporation of women into the armed forces, we do not agree that women have to have the same role as men, within the military, as we believe that these roles are not appropriate. We believe that the military academy is not a good place for women. In fact, it is not a good place for anybody.

From a gender perspective, an important way in which militarism affects us are the values, values which are deeply rooted in culture and within the militias – and these are values which we want to put an end to. We want to put an end to military culture in schools, in the streets, in the home, everywhere. In the country, both men and women are affected by militarism, as there is repression of social struggles, be it a struggle which defends women's rights or any other rights, and this repression is even worse in rural areas. However, when it comes to military values, it is often women who suffer more than men, as this is a very machista country. Even nowadays, despite efforts being made by many organisations to change the situation, machismo is still a very common practice not only amongst men or within institutions which promote these sorts of values, such as the armed forces, but also amongst women, especially those living in rural areas. Here are just a few examples to illustrate my point better.

Household chores are always carried out by women; women must always serve men. Young girls are taught that they have to do the domestic chores and that they need to serve men from childhood onwards – for example, serving brothers, and this is endorsed by the majority of society and people are surprised if a man, for example, washes his own clothes or carries out household chores if they are living with their partner, with a woman or with their mother or sister. In general, this is seen as strange or the woman is considered as lazy.

The same thing happens in terms of sexual freedom: if men enjoy themselves, they are idolised and praised, whereas if a woman does the same she is considered to be a woman without morals. One must recognise that this situation has improved in the capital and in more urban areas, but this is still a common attitude in the countryside.

As a final example, in terms of women's civil status when they are married, once they get married women automatically have to adopt the husband's surname. If you do not want to adopt the surname, you have to officially declare that you do not wish to use it and only once this official declaration has been made can you continue to use your own maiden name. This is ridiculous because everyone identifies who you are based on your name and you should be comfortable with your own name and therefore women should have the right to choose their identity.

Finally, I want to say that in recent years, there have been more women than men in MOC. We looked at the possibility of creating a separate antimilitarist feminist group and we decided that it was not necessary to separate ourselves from our male colleagues in order to discuss feminism or antimilitarism because we believe that we can address these issues together and carry out projects within MOC.

Thanks to Francesca Denley for translation from Spanish to English

References

[1] *"The president of Paraguay confirms that a conflict with Bolivia is possible inorder to justify the increase in military budget"*. http://www.rebelion.org/noticia.php?id=37547
[2] http://elyacare.wordpress.com/2008/01/23/denuncian-en-paraguay-atropellos-a-asentamientos-campesinos/
[3] This declaration is presented along with the article.
[4] This declaration is presented along with the article.

Brief history of the Antimilitarist Movement in Paraguay

The story of MOC (Movimiento de Objeción de Conciencia — Conscientious Objection Movement) goes back to 1981, demanding the elimination of obligatory military service. The initial intention was to ask for the abolition of military service, but then this changed to calling for the recognition of conscientious objection, as a transition proposal.

- In 1992 the Constituent Convention approved in very restrictive terms an article on conscientious objection relating to military service.
- In 1993, the first objectors' group was set up. With the support of Serpaj-Paraguay, antimilitarist training was expanded. The first presentation was prepared, support groups were trained, a communication strategy was drawn up, etc. There was great fear of a repressive legal or illegal reaction. Later that year the first group of five objectors presented themselves and achieved impressive media coverage. The military preferred not to react against the emergence of this first group of objectors.

- In 1994 there was a second group, of seven conscientious objectors.
- MOC was founded on 17 August, and the third group of objectors declared themselves, made up of five objectors and the first female objector. The Human Rights Commission of the Chamber of Deputies decided to receive all the declarations of conscientious objection and to hand in written evidence of these declarations. It was at this point that the Conscientious Objection Movement (MOC) was created.
- 24 July 1995 – the Day of the Army and inauguration of the parade of general Lino Oviedo. Direct actions of MOC and other political groups were carried out during the ceremony and there was strong repression enacted by the military and the police.
- On 9 August the group of women antimilitarists of MOC presented themselves (see the declaration on page 127).
- On 15 December MOC received the Memorial Prize for Peace and Solidarity with the People, which was awarded by Nobel Prize winner Adolfo Pérez Esquivel.
- In 1996, with the help of MOC, the National Worker's Centre launched the campaign "Enough of compulsory military service").
- In 1997, forced recruitment in rural zones within the country gained strength. The churches demanded legislation for the right to conscientious objection with wide-ranging guarantees.
- In October 1997, 81 social and campesino organisations called on Congress to reduce its military spending by 25%, while the 1998 budget was being drawn up. .

Thanks to Francesca Denley for translation from Spanish to English

Presentation of Women Conscientious Objectors in Paraguay, 1995

Press Communiqué

On Wednesday, 9 August, a group of 11 women will publicly present themselves as CONSCIENTIOUS OBJECTORS at 8.30am in front of the Human Rights Commission. In Paraguay there are already 8 women who have previously presented themselves as objectors, but this is the first group made up of only women. We would like to therefore express the motives behind our objection:

We object to military service which promotes a machista image. This image is of men as macho, strong, insensitive, who can deal with anything, the warrior, who is educated so as to deal with a tough life "outside of the home". This is totally contrary to the image of women, who are considered weak, naïve, educated to serve in the home, and be the main source of support for the warrior. They are expected to simply serve men.

We object to the army as it is the armed branch of this system, which is based on all sorts of injustices in which a few hoard the wealth and exploit the great majority whilst ensuring that the majority remain living in poverty. We object to militarism, which impregnates all values in society, such as obedience in the face of creativity, arrogance towards others, chauvinism/machismo regarding relations between the sexes, violence as opposed to dialogue in conflict resolution, submission as opposed to responsibility and self-control, authoritarianism as opposed to freedom and liberty, etc...

In order to limit the increase of militarism, as women we need to be able to create new alternative social ways of thinking through participation in cultural, social and political spaces, which promote values such as mutual trust, solidarity, cooperation, etc. We need spaces in which decisions are made based on consensus, whereby self-criticism allows us to stop reproducing ways of thinking which involve any sort of marginalisation. We call for men to take into consideration their chauvinist-"machista" practices, roles and values which they impose on us. They should reflect on their behaviour and make adjustments where necessary. We want women to become aware of the discrimination which we suffer, and we will unite so as to demonstrate our strength and gain dignity as women in our society.

There is no possibility of real change in human and social relations without women participating in these changes. It is therefore necessary for women to participate in the antimilitarist struggle so as to be able to start creating, from now on, a just society so as to achieve freedom for women.

MUJERES ANTIMILITARISTAS — MOC

Thanks to Francesca Denley for translation from Spanish to English

Presentation of Women Objectors and Antimilitarists

Antimilitarist Women from the Conscientious Objectors Movement of Paraguay (25 May 2002)

Within the framework of International Conscientious Objectors' Day, the antimilitarist women's group from MOC-Paraguay presented the third group of women objectors. Around 25 women refused to participate in military service and, above all, rejected the armed forces as an institution representing the patriarchal culture. This act also seeks to demonstrate how the push for integration of women into the official institutional framework is actually being rejected by a significant sector of society. Please find below the protest as expressed by our colleagues.

"Because equality is not merely a question of space"

So as to mark International Conscientious Objectors' Day, the antimilitarist women of MOC, in our third presentation, declare ourselves as conscientious objectors to a system represented by a culture of economic, social and cultural oppression of men against men and women against women.

We object to occupying spaces which do not create positive alternatives for the promotion of female participation, given that the inclusion of women in the military is merely used as a justification for an increase in the budget of an institution whose only role in our country is to corrupt and steal.

We therefore state that militarism is not only a problem relating to gender. It is a social problem which implies the perpetuation of a whole set of values which are vertical and authoritarian in nature. This would therefore represent a setback in our struggle for a demilitarised and democratic society.

We do not believe in the armed forces as an institution, given that they are based on violence and a patriarchal culture, and we therefore refuse to be a part of this structure.

Conscientious objection is a universal right. We are objectors, not objects.

Thanks to Francesca Denley for translation from Spanish to English

Introduction to Colombia

Colombia is a country characterised by daily violence and enormous differences between poor and rich. The country is highly militarised, and a civil war has been going on for more than 40 years. Both the government army, the FARC guerillas (*Fuerzas Armadas Revolucionarias de Colombia* — Revolutionary Armed Forces of Colombia) and the ELN guerillas (*Ejército de Liberación Nacional* — National Liberation Army), and the paramilitaries, are all very present in society, committing violence and recruiting young people. Militarism is reflecting Colombian patriarchy. Only men are conscripted to the government army, but in the name of gender equality women are recruited to both the guerilla groups and to the paramilitaries. Because of this situation in Colombian society, women within the antimilitarist movement declare themselves as conscientious objectors, objecting to militarism in its broad sense.

We present here a contribution by *Andrea Ochoa* on women as conscientious objectors, and several declarations of women conscientious objectors.

Introduction by Ellen Elster, War Resisters' International

Women Conscientious Objectors in Colombia

By Andrea Ochoa, Acción Colectiva de Objetores y Objetoras de Conciencia

I t was back in 1924 that there was the first instance of women objecting to compulsory military service. Union leader Carlota Rua, during the first Workers' Congress, opened the debate on the obligation of military service by arguing that young workers and peasants should not be taken from their land, where they contributed to the country with their work, to be forced into destroying it as part of the army. This same initiative prompted another group of women to oppose the recruitment of their sons and husbands during the war against Peru, making their objection public and generating debate inside the country [1].

As the years have passed, women have continued to organise initiatives against the internal war, in search of peace and solutions to the armed conflict, based on mediation. It is worth mentioning the efforts of the working group *"Women and Armed Conflict"*, which brings together diverse organisations and individuals to investigate and question the multiple forms of violence that affect women, young women and girls in the context of the armed conflict in Colombia — work highly relevant as gender violence was invisible, despite the harshness of violent acts against the female gender by the different armed actors [2].

Equally important is the work of the Alliance *"Colombian Women's Initiatives for Peace"*, again bringing groups together on the basis of UN Security Council Resolution 1325 (approved 31 October 2000) calling for the participation of women's groups in negotiations and dialogue about armed conflict and for recognition of their contribution to processes of reconciliation and reducing the impact of armed conflict on women [3]. These organisations have carried out important work, intervening in political debate, as well as engaging in social work and public demonstrations.

In our country, where only men are obliged to do military service, the position of women has gone far beyond solidarity with friends, partners or sons, to contribute work and initiatives in the construction of a Colombia that is learning to transform its conflicts without resort to violence, a Colombia more equitable and without the sharp social injustices that fuel all the country's problems. From this point of view, the work on conscientious objection has especially spread through the development of an alternative pedagogy, reaching out to children, youth and adults of all social and cultural traditions with its promotion of nonviolence. At the same time, it has extended its perspectives to address themes such as the injustice of excessive charges for public services, the importance of fair trade (trade that is just, conscious and in solidarity), and the creativity of direct action. In these areas of work, women have made a vital contribution.

It is also relevant to note that as well as the state's system of conscription, groups outside the law — such as guerrillas and paramilitaries — recruit, both coercively and voluntarily, men and women under the banner of gender equality. This is why it has been so important to have women declare themselves as conscientious objectors, refusing to participate in any army or contribute in any way to the machisto, patriarchal and militarist culture that maintains the harsh violence Colombia suffers.

In this way, women within the conscientious objector movement in Colombia have made it possible to take up both the problem and the proposed alternatives to war from a broad perspective, understanding the complexity of Colombian reality and the need to propose deep and structural alternatives. It is touching that we are the ones who have most power to call people to take part in public acts and that men, besides feeling supported in their refusal of military service, recognise us as equally important within the movement, knowing that everybody needs to commit themselves sould, heart and hands in the transformation of everyday life and the policies that support war.

This text was first printed in The Broken Rifle No 74, May 2007. It has been edited for this anthology.

Footnotes

[1] Giraldo, Jhon. *"La Objeción de Conciencia en Colombia: una historia en movimiento"* published at http://www.nodo50.org/moc-carabanchel/campa%F1as/objecion/15m04_colombia_agresion.htm
[2] Web page of Mesa de Mujer y Conflicto Armado en Colombia http://www.mujeryconflictoarmado.org/lamesa.html
[3] Web page of Iniciativa Mujeres por la Paz: http://www.mujeresporlapaz.org/

Women Objectors in the Colombian Context

Alejandra Londoño Bustamante, Red Juvenil de Medellín

I am a conscientious objector, but not because I believe that objection is a refusal which has legal backing. On the contrary, it is a legitimate social and collective organisation which initially aims at change within individuals for the good of society.

I refuse to continue reproducing the patriarchal practices which support inequality and exclusion. I am not an objector because I fear that my son or my brother will go off to war. I am an objector as a woman because, even though I am not wielding a gun, I could still be contributing to the reproduction of patriarchal tradition which places women in a submissive role. These practices destroy women's dreams and their capacity to decide, have an opinion and act. They are denied pleasure and they are placed in a position of servitude towards others. As conscientious objector, I am trying to change the everyday elements which go unnoticed amidst the gunfire. I am also trying to change my immediate personal environment. This is essentially an environment which allows for the continued use of weapons.

I constantly hear questions from soldiers and the general population, who ask, "Why are there women objectors, given that it is the men who go off to war?" It is precisely over this point that we have the most strength in claiming that this is not a demand restricted to men. Objection is not merely a proposal which arises from an armed conflict. It is a clear way of demonstrating a popular, nonviolent struggle, which states that in order for the desired changes to take place, a change needs to happen at an individual level. It is a continuing question when looking at ways in which to create power with and for everybody.

Thanks to Francesca Denley for translation from Spanish to English

Sandra Murillo Marín's Declaration

I declare myself as a conscientious objector because I do not believe that peace can be achieved through weapons and violence (irrespective of who practises it). I do not believe that repression, obeying orders, violating human rights, and defending the interests of those in power is the right path to take. All the military structures, both legal and illegal, merely maintain the patriarchal position which oppresses us and does not allow us to progress alongside other people, who want to implement change for the good of society and not just for a small minority. I make this declaration because I no longer want to see violent deaths, massacres, arrests — amongst other things — which are carried out by those who call themselves defenders of human rights.

I declare myself a conscientious objector because I want to invest in society instead of investing in this wretched war.

I want to be free and see others working together as a people for the common interests, and not see them as my enemies.

Sandra Murillo Marín, 11 February 2007 .

Thanks to Francesca Denley for translation from Spanish to English

134

Estefanía Gómez Vásquez's Declaration

How does one speak of adopting a political stance in a heartbreaking context, which is consumed by violence and based on the elimination of the other in order to guarantee one's own survival? How does one address the war-driven economy and injustice? How does one criticise a government and media which sells us peace through war. How can I make a distinction between myself and those who are indifferent towards the Columbian conflict and the sadly human desire to find pleasure in a power which involves prejudice, poverty, resignation and fear of others? How do I define myself as a conscientious objector, and expand a debate within a country and its dominating ideologies, without recognising that this history and ideology are intrinsically part of my own background? How do I do all this without first recognizing that I have more personal reasons, rather than just political, social and economic ones, for deciding to go against this system and not conform, so as to speak out and feel the need to propose and develop alternatives for those who, like me, believe that things can be different. That we do not need to count on war and that our bodies are not merely machines of death.

Describing my situation may be simpler than I thought. It is simply about wanting to see and feel different things, to be part of this different reality and to believe that, with every day that passes, the criticism made will never work unless a proposal for change is made. The discussions need to satisfy people's expectations. It is often the case that we do not carry through all that has been said, and this is what I want to change. Actions speak louder than words and so we should work silently but constructively. I wish that my actions did not need words in order to be considered as part of the debate.

And so my conscientious objection is not about limiting myself to merely being against the system, neither am I simply against a war which goes completely beyond my actions and my very being. I simply do not want to be part of those whose work involves following the ravages caused by the war, picking up the remaining pieces and, without achieving much, try to make it sustainable, thereby paving the way for the same thing to happen again. I would like to have a moral job in this world. Therefore I reject more than the war, I reject indifference and desperation, and those who merely stand by and do nothing or those who are happy to talk without actually doing anything. I choose to be critically aware and constantly striving for change.

Being a conscientious objector means inscribing a different history on my body. It means showing, through each of my actions, how war is not the way through which I wish to relate to others. It shows that competition does not feed my desire for power. Power is precisely about leaving open questions, about opening new paths, serving as an example — thus showing others that they can believe, and know that it is possible to go beyond the complaints and indifference and belief that this is the way things will always be. I am showing that I, and others, can disobey a certain context in order to follow their personal conviction.

This declaration is made in a moment of urgency, so as to say that I do not intend to give in. My body and mind will resist the barrage of opinions which, as a whole, tries to buy me, impose itself upon me and justify itself to me. This space is mine and I have the duty and right to this space in the world, and to do with it, what I consider irreparable and imminent ... believing in myself and other people who think beyond themselves as individuals, believing in those who share the same challenge as I am facing. I want to show that it is easier to ignore something when you are an invisible victim of a board game for those who make us believe that we are playing in favour of life and justice, because I am playing for myself, for what I believe in and what I feel; because being invisible is not a consolation and much less a privilege. I am here for those who wish to listen to me and who stop and think for a second about how many things in their life have been based on decisions made by them or for them. For me, my conscientious objection is an example of one such occasion.

Estefanía Gómez Vásquez, November 2007

Thanks to Francesca Denley for translation from Spanish to English

I Declare My Objection

The fact that I am a girl — and bear in mind that in this country being a girl is very different to being a boy — does not mean that we are spared the effects of the war, authoritarianism, militarisation of society and social, economic and political policies.

In fact, it is us women who, more than others, are subjected to a culture of silence, which educates through submission and servitude and above all submits to authoritarianism, discrimination, control, fear, repression, the implementation of hierarchy, degradation, impoverishment, exclusion and commercialisation. All these aspects deny us our being. As women we are spuriously made to believe that we are to abide by the law.

Furthermore, we must suffer witnessing our brothers, uncles, cousins, friends and strangers who, in order to guarantee the liberties of the people, end up joining an army where they learn to hate, mistreat, stop feeling, stop being human. In the end they are not those who are protecting the rights of "our country" but, on the contrary, they are the very people who are responsible for restricting these freedoms. A friend, uncle, cousin, acquaintance, whom we do not see for a year or a year and a half, depending on the context, because, in such cases, we are not all equal. They receive training and a life experience which does not make up for the solitude, insecurity, anxiety, terror, cold-hearted attitude and humiliation experienced ...

Fortunately, and I say this with all my being, some of my relatives chose not to serve in the compulsory military service. Did they do this for reasons relating to conscientious objection? I do not know. However, what I do know is that, rather than sacrifice an important part of their lives merely because it is compulsory, they preferred to protect their lives. They preferred to work, study, love, feel and be human.

As a woman and speaking from the difficult position of being a woman, I DECLARE MYSELF A CONSCIENTIOUS OBJECTOR. Not only do I reject the existence of armies, such as those in my country; I also declare myself as an objector to this economic, social and cultural model. I oppose the security policies which are being implemented on a global level, where war practices are degrading and the human being has become a puppet which can be destroyed.

I resoundingly reject a model which excludes us and I refuse to participate in this imposed submission, in a world which tells me what to do and constantly degrades me as a woman. I oppose this patriarchy, this hierarchy ...

I demand a different world, a completely different one, for my mum, my dad, my brothers and sisters, friends, neighbours, farmers, dogs, cats, plants and mother earth. We all have the right to live in dignity where there is justice and respect. For those of us who are human with freedom of conscience, fully aware of not obeying, I declare myself thus, as I do not want to obey ...

Milena Romero Sanabria

Thanks to Francesca Denley for translation from Spanish to English

Women's Conscientious Objection as a Strategy Against Militarism — Concluding Remarks From The Editors

By Ellen Elster and Majken Jul Sørensen, War Resisters' International

In this concluding chapter we will discuss the different themes that the texts in this book have brought up. In the introduction we suggested that conscientious objection can exist both in a broad and a narrow understanding of it, and here we will explore this further. We see that most women who choose to declare themselves conscientious objectors are working in the mixed conscientious objection movement. There could be at least two reasons for this. One is to make women's perspectives on militarism more visible within the male-dominated organisation. The other reason is to make conscientious objection a strategy against militarism. This strategy will often be consistent with the strategy in women-only organisations [1]. Within both types of organisation, women stress the contradiction between feminism and militarism. Part of this is the debate on conscription for women, a debate which arises from time to time where women's emancipation is a central question. Then, we take a look at the future. What strikes us is women breaking away from the traditional nurturing role within the mixed conscientious objection movement to a clear and radical feminist critique of militarism. This might pave the way for men conscientious objectors to include a gender perspective into their critique of militarism, a perspective which is often not part of men's antimilitarism.

Broad and Narrow Understandings of Conscientious Objection

In the introduction we briefly indicated a difference between "narrow" and "broad" conscientious objection. A narrow understanding of conscientious objection is the refusal to participate in compulsory military training or service. A broad understanding of conscientious objection goes way beyond this. In this case, both men and women object to militarism and its influence on society and all aspects of the military system, refusing to participate in any kind of activity which can be associated with the military system. In some places people who are conscientious objectors in the narrow sense are required to do "civilian" or unarmed alternative service instead. People who refuse alternative service are called "total objectors". As we have seen from the stories told here, the broad understanding of conscientious objection is not a recent phenomenon. The articles from Sweden and Britain are examples of this. It is the broad definition of conscientious objection that the War Resisters' International has been promoting for many years. The question is where the line should be drawn. Are all types of peace work part of being a conscientious objector? We don't think so, because then conscientious objection becomes too broad and loose to have meaning.

What we can see from the texts in this book is that women who declare themselves conscientious objectors in our broad understanding of the term do two things simultaneously. First, they take a personal stand. As an individual, they say, *"I'm a conscientious objector"*. At the same time, they object to militarism and the militarisation of society, not just to a certain kind of service which affects them personally. It is an interesting paradox, that feminists who stress the importance of collective responsibility for the world choose such an individual act as their method. Conscientious objection is something that originated in *"western"* thinking and is linked to the same set of ideas as human rights, which also emphasise the importance of the individual. Of course, the women build a bridge between the individual and the group when they encourage other women (and men) to take a similar stand, thereby making the individual refusal a condition for collective resistance to militarism. One of the challenges we see from the texts is how to distinguish women's conscientious objection activities from other female activities in the peace movement. A natural consequence of making a personal stand against all aspects of militarism is to become involved in other types of peace work which challenge militarism. Naturally enough, the women who tell their stories here do not make a clear distinction between their *"conscientious objection"* and their *"other peace work"*, because one is closely linked to the other.

Broad and narrow understandings of refusal seem to exist side by side. That the understanding did not start narrow and then turn broader over the years we see from the fact that the Swedish women were taking a much more radical stand earlier than the others. We think this broad understanding of the term *"conscientious objection"* is present in many of the stories, either implicitly or explicitly. It is clear for *Barbro Alving* in the Swedish case, and for the British absolutists during World War II. They used the term absolutists when they also refused to do alternative work, which included not only conscription to the military and work in the military-industrial sector, but also alternative civil work. The reason was that this would release men for active military service. The same situation applied for women in the US, though they were not conscripted. In support of men's conscientious objection and helping them in practical ways, the women regarded this as a positive act against militarism. The stories we hear from World War II, both from Britain and the United States, are usually from women who already had a strong pacifist and antimilitarist conviction, and who had participated in antimilitarist work even before the war. Now, in many countries which are involved in wars but don't have conscription, we find a growing number of women who develop an antimilitarist attitude while serving in the military. So there is no reason to think that these women did not exist during WWII. They have just not had an opportunity to tell their story.

Israel and Eritrea are today the two countries with military service for women. When women refuse service, they become conscientious objectors in the narrow sense.

The same thing can be said for women in the USA who have joined the army *"voluntarily"*. Leaving the army, before their period of service has ended, for reason of conscience is extremely difficult, but they have the opportunity to apply for conscientious objector status and be a conscientious objector in the narrow sense. This is the legal way of doing it, but as we have seen *Stephanie Atkinson* chose to go AWOL, and she was later sentenced for that. *Stephanie Atkinson*'s piece is an excellent illustration of how to differentiate between a broad and narrow understanding of conscientious objection and how complicated this is. This is because she uses the term conscientious objection the way the US army does, and the US army only gives this status to a very limited number of the people who want to leave the military for reasons of conscience. However, both *Stephanie Atkinson* and *Diedra Cobb* are examples of what we call conscientious objectors in the broad sense.

In many European countries both with and without conscription, women can join the military *"voluntarily"*, which also means that there is a potential for women conscientious objectors in the narrow sense in Europe. From Finland we know of a few cases. In this country, women can join voluntarily, but after a 45-day trial period it becomes obligatory to finish the service. A few women in Finland have applied for conscientious objector status after the 45 days and done the rest of their service as a civilian substitute service following the same laws as male conscripts. But in 2009, a woman who wishes to remain anonymous became a total objector when she refused both to complete her military service and the substitute service because she considered the *"civilian"* service a continuation of the military system. She will probably be sentenced to two weeks in prison [2].

But even women who are conscientious objectors in the narrow sense can be defined as objectors in the broad sense, when they object to militarism as a whole, and not just to their own service. *Idan Halili* of Israel is a clear example of this kind of objector. Our understanding is that women who are conscientious objectors in the broad sense would have become total objectors had they had to do an *"alternative service"*.

A Feminist Confrontation with Militarism

Many of the writings in this book argue for a broad understanding of conscientious objection because they see militarism as a contrast to feminist values and a contradiction to women's interests in society. Not everyone uses the word *"feminist"* or *"feminism"*, but they clearly use their identity as women for their arguments against militarism — *Barbro Alving* is such a case. In Israel we see a development of the reasons for being a conscientious objector from religion, conscience, then politics and now including a feminist stand, like *Shani Werner* and *Idan Halili*.

Idan Halili was the first woman in Israel openly refusing on feminist grounds, which led to a prison-sentence. Her argument was that the feminist approach clashes with violent ways of solving problems. The military system harms women both within the army and in society at large. She claims that enlistment means agreeing to be part of a system that is based on relations of power and control. It systematically perpetuates the exclusion of women from the public sphere and constructs their place in society as secondary to men. She doesn't want to serve *"just like a man"*, since she is not looking for a kind of equality which reinforces the privileges enjoyed by men. *Idan Halili* does not want to participate in an organisation which is fundamentally and by definition not equal, and which is in sharp contrast to her ideological principles and conscience. As a feminist, Idan Halili declares that it is her obligation to build civil alternatives to the army through which she and other feminists can make their contribution to society, which includes striving to reduce the influence of the army.

Although *Idan Halili* and the other Israeli women are in a special situation since they in fact are conscripted, we still think that she speaks for many of the other women in this book. Even if their background and situation vary greatly, they all link the culture of the military with the current hierarchical power structure and patriarchy. They take a broad stand against militarism, pointing at the damage it does to women and society as a whole. It is reflected in the statement from 1980 where women declared themselves as total resisters, stating that emancipation had nothing to do with militarism. The French women in 1991 point at the army's male domination, which reproduces the patriarchal model in society. In Turkey, *Ferda Ülker* describes the traditional view of women in relation to the military only as mothers, sisters, wives, and girlfriends of the boys who will become soldiers. *Hilal Demir* adds that there's a risk of becoming *"masculinised"*, with the effect that the feminist perspective is overlooked in the mixed conscientious objection movement. This has to be seen in the context of Turkish society which is highly militarised, and where women are clearly marginalised. This is also the case in Korea.

Moving to Latin America, the Paraguayan and Colombian women describe their societies and their reasons for declaring themselves as conscientious objectors in the same way, seeing the armed forces as promoting the violent culture of their society, by preserving militarism, patriarchy, machismo, submission and outright war. The military also uphold the structures of injustice, human rights abuse and exploitation of resources that result in poverty for the majority of people. Women within the conscientious objection movement in Colombia propose alternatives to war from a broad perspective, understanding the complexity of Colombian reality. *Andrea Ochoa* argues that women are the ones who have most power to call people to take part in public actions.

Since a feminist critique of militarism is also a confrontation with patriarchy and its consequences, it is logical that feminist refusers also raise the question of "heroism". Often members of the conscientious objection movement consider men or women who have to go to prison for refusing military service as heroes. *Idan Halili* finds this problematic, seeing it as a continuation of a militaristic pattern which makes heroes of men who make sacrifices — in this case, conscientious objectors who sacrifice their personal freedom for a principle. She refuses to be considered a hero for her refusal. After serving one prison term, she realises that she is not giving up her principles by accepting a discharge on the military's terms and not her own, for she is following her own feminist principles by refusing to become a hero. *Ferda Ülker* also reflects on the tendency to compare the risks of female and male conscientious objectors. Men who have to serve prison terms easily become heroes of the movement. She thinks that by making these comparisons and participating in this "hero game", women serve the cause of militarism. *Hilal Demir* says that refusal of military service by men, and their subsequent "heroism", may accelerate the movement to some degree; but succeeding strategies should aim to avoid this "heroism", which is both a male and a militarist concept that we should criticise.

A related problem is raised by *Diedra Cobb*. Although she did not spend time in prison, she had the feeling that the activist groups who assisted her during the process of getting out of the military were not interested in her as a human being, but as a case which could be used to promote their groups' interests. *Diedra Cobb* does not discuss this in the context of feminism, but we think it is another example of how the military's dehumanisation is also affecting the peace movement.

The women's stories about conscientious objection add a wider perspective to the concept of conscientious objection, whether it is seen in connection with refusing military service, or women declaring themselves as conscientious objectors outside the legal framework. But all the women give a feminist dimension to the concept. They all point at the military as an institution which is oppressive in its structure and values, and how these are imposed on the society at large, and how masculinity is a very integrated part of it. As a natural consequence of this, almost all of the women are also supporters of men's conscientious objectors, as we have seen clearly in the examples from Turkey and Korea. An intriguing exception from this is the case from Germany, were many of the people who objected to women's involvement in the military in the 1970s and 1980s did not question conscription for men, and therefore did not question the military system as a whole.

Why Become a Conscientious Objector when There is no Conscription?

The question of why women declare themselves conscientious objectors when they are not subject to conscription is central to this book. We think that the answer lies both within the women's own organisations, and their effort to confront militarism, as well as from their understanding of the wider society they are part of. How they react to things happening in their own organisations is influenced by what happens in the wider society, and *vice versa*.

The evidence indicates that it is women in mixed peace groups who primarily declare themselves conscientious objectors, not women who are active in women-only organisations. There are several women's peace organisations and groups with a clear feminist stand, such as *Women in Black, Ruta Pacifica* (Colombia), and *Women's International League for Peace and Freedom*. These groups choose other ways than conscientious objection to express their resistance to militarism and they do not have a logical place this book.

The women in mixed groups have had a need to find their own place as women in these organisations, based on their understanding of militarism and their experiences as women, especially from the 1970s onwards. A declaration as a conscientious objector became one of the answers to this. With the women's liberation movement in the 1970s and 1980s the discussion about being women in the mixed and male-dominated peace movement started. Many peace organisations were mostly based on men's conscientious objection and total resistance, and the WRI was certainly part of this debate. Women refused *"to be coffee makers"* and to *"keep the homefires burning"* while the men were serving prison sentences for conscientious objection. Women wanted to be part of the peace movement in their own right. From this basis women in WRI declared themselves as total resisters in 1980. The women were active at international WRI meetings, insisting that women's work and women's resistance to war were not only about helping the conscientious objectors. Many women have experienced invisibility because they are women among a majority of men. Their need for a space of their own and for raising issues from women's perspectives have, in many cases, not been respected. As we have seen above, a feminist analysis shows that war and militarism affects women in a variety of ways, and often it is different from men's experiences. Conscientious objection may be a concept which mainly affect men, in a legal sense, but it has effects on non-conscripted women as well, because of the way patriarchy is sustaining militarism.

In countries where women are conscripted, they meet many of the same challenges within their movement as women who don't face conscription. *Shani Werner*, from Israel, points out that, in her experience, men conscientious objectors are imprisoned while women get exempted from service. This was a way of militarising draft resistance, she felt. Women's conscientious objection remains then personal, or silenced, or — as she calls it — a *"coffee serving resistance"*. In Turkey, men try to explain women's presence in the conscientious objector movement only by their relationship to and support of a male conscientious objector. Women conscientious objectors reject this view as typically male. Although they do support men's refusal of compulsory service, they primarily try to make militarism visible and show how it penetrates all sectors of social life and social relations. One argument against women declaring themselves conscientious objectors is that, by doing this, the women implicitly accept the logic of conscription and the military system. Is it possible to reject the system by adopting its way of viewing the world? Why don't the women call themselves war resisters or antimilitarists rather than conscientious objectors? This can easily be done by a letter writing campaign or public declarations. Why is it attractive to adopt a term that is integrated into the military system? *Stephanie Atkinson* is implicitly supporting this when she says that she prefers to identify herself as a proud deserter rather than as a conscientious objector.

Hilal Demir says that many think that the term *"objection"* is invented for legal situations created by compulsory military service. It follows from this reasoning that, if women don't have to do military service, they cannot object to it. But she distinguishes between a legal framework and the broader understanding of conscientious objection discussed previously. As *Hilal Demir* says, women can change the meaning of terms by developing them. The question is whether the conscientious objection platform is the right place. She thinks that conscientious objection declarations by 12 women led to both greater gender sensitivity within the movement and challenged the discussions on this concept. There is a need for not only making women visible in the mixed conscientious objector movement, but also for consciousness raising both among the women themselves, and the men. *Hilal Demir* thinks that everyone needs to understand that women will have their own reasons for joining the movement, and that both women's and men's perspectives need to be considered.

Unlike Turkey, there is no opposition to women objectors in Paraguay, according to *Maria Elena Meza Barboza*. At some point in the movement's history, there were more women than men, which gave the movement legitimacy. Women have the same say, and decision-making is by consensus. The adverse reactions to women's conscientious objection come from the outside, and most critics do not recognise how militarism affects women in serious ways.

As we have seen, reactions within the organisations and movements where women participate vary a great deal. But internal dynamics are only one explanation of why women decide to become conscientious objectors. It is primarily a strategy of action directed towards the wider society. This raises the question of whether conscientious objection is a good strategy for women's confrontation with militarism. Is this an effective method of reaching out to other people to explain what antimilitarism is all about? Or do the resisters run the risk that the lack of comprehension will remain? Are the opportunities for communication lost because the women distance themselves from the mainstream peace movement? The contributors to this anthology have obviously found stronger arguments in favour of declarations than against. The Turkish women have argued that the questions that women's conscientious objection raise have been a good opportunity to enter into dialogue about antimilitarism. At least people are asking questions, though finding the reasons difficult to understand. Korean women also say that people outside the conscientious objector movement don't understand why women engage in military issues. The Korean women are not declaring themselves as conscientious objectors, but have chosen a strategy together with the men in the movement to show the suffering, not only of the conscientious objector, but also of the network around him, including the women. This is a way to break the silence of women's voices on this matter, says *Jung-min Choi*.

The Norwegian sociologist *Thomas Mathiesen* [3] has written about how movements that work for social change can be successful. One of his findings is that organisations that are good at making their voices heard and understood balance on the thin edge between being drawn into the mainstream — thereby losing their radical stand — and being considered an outcast that no-one needs to take seriously. In this way of thinking, what will work regarding women's conscientious objection in places where they are not conscripted will depend a great deal on the circumstances, and on the women's ability to communicate with the rest of society.

One thing which becomes obvious when looking at this collection of stories is how important it is to understand women's conscientious objection as a reaction to what is happening around these contributors. Objection does not happen in a vacuum: it is always a reaction to outside circumstances, and what constitutes the context. As already discussed, women are reacting to militarism, and they are often also responding to the internal dynamics of their own organisations. But when that is said, there are also other contexts which need to be taken into consideration. One context is the broader peace movement in that particular country. As we understand it, the objectors are not only objecting to militarism, but many times also to the usual way of understanding and *"doing"* peace work, which they don't consider personal and radical enough. A second context that the conscientious objectors have to place themselves in is the feminist movement, and how people who call themselves feminists perceive militarism. That views on the military differ is clear from the case of fighter pilot-to-be *Alice Miller* in Israel. The third context is the *"ordinary"* society, and the understanding of militarism in that society. Some women live in countries where militarism is very visible and penetrating much of everyday society, whereas other women live where militarism is much less obvious. Judgments about the effectiveness of women's conscientious objection have to include evaluations of how they are accepted in all three contexts, as well as their effect on their own organisations.

Why is Conscription for Women Incompatible with Radical Feminism?

Military values are contradictory to feminism and the values women contributors hope to see in society. Both the stories from the US and Eritrea show how military life affects women who get involved in the army. These women tell of sexual abuse in an environment that has no respect for diversity and human life. But also, women who have never been enrolled in the military articulate arguments of why the military is not compatible with radical feminism. Their stories on why they chose to declare themselves as conscientious objectors can also be regarded as arguments against conscription of women. The Israeli contributions raise this question when they mention *Alice Miller*, who was one of the first to demand the same rights for women as men in the military when she wanted to become a fighter pilot. It was argued that access to the most important combat roles, often a precondition for other high-ranking positions in the military, would give women access to other influential positions in society, which again would reduce oppression of women. This question was also central in Europe in the late 1970s and during the 1980s, in fact until the so-called cold war ended. Another Alice, *Alice Schwarzer* from West Germany, became a symbol of the debate in Europe at the time, when she launched the idea that conscription of women was necessary in order for women to get into the highest places of power, which were completely male-dominated. *Alice Schwarzer* was the editor of the feminist magazine *Emma*, highly respected for its radicalism, and a voice for women's emancipation. Therefore her declaration came as a surprise for women in the antimilitarist movement.

The WRI women's statement from 1980 took a clear stand against the incorporation of women into the military, rejecting the emancipation of women through adopting men's roles. They had seen, through history, how women had been drawn into the military and then out again, according to the needs of the military. An example of this was World War II where British women were encouraged to take the men's jobs and were even conscripted to the army, only to be sent back to the kitchen once the war was over. In an article in *Spare Rib* [4] in 1981 called *"Equality in the Army – No Way!"*, *Lesley Merryfinch* writes that women took men's place in the munitions factories and other significant industries. Even child-minding was official war-work. Women who participated in liberation armies, for example the Eritrean liberation army, had similar experiences. The stories of *Ruta Yosef-Tudla* and *Bisrat Habte Micael* discredit arguments that military service endows a high degree of liberation for women, although women became involved in this army in the name of gender equality. *Lesley Merryfinch* also mentions Germany, where women were conscripted to do health-work in the military at the end of the 1970s. This inspired many actions by radical feminists protesting through demonstrations and a postcard campaign, as described in the contribution from Germany.

Other voices within the feminist movement, both today and in the past, point to sexual harassment as the norm in the military. In the US, women have openly reported sexual harassment and rape by their male colleagues [5]. Introducing the US section, *Joanne Sheehan* noted that, while many women have had traumatic experiences of sexual assault, only very few want to talk about this — it is just too painful. *Diedra Cobb* writes of experiencing sexual assault, without taking the issue further. As *Idan Halili* argues, if women are to succeed militarily, they will have to adjust to the norm of the combat soldier, *"the fighting man"*, and they are expected to conform to an image which is powerfully identified with stereotypical masculinity.

The debate about conscription for women today continues in some countries, and the positions for and against conscription have not changed much. *Tali Lerner* writes about the debate in Israel.

A comparable debate has been a burning issue in Norway during the past five to ten years. Men are still conscripted in Norway, although the number of professional soldiers is increasing in order to serve as part of NATO and European forces in other parts of the world. At the same time, there is a serious debate about introducing conscription for women — not because of lack of personnel (in fact only one in four of male potential conscripts serve), but in the name of gender equality. A generation gap seems to influence views on this issue. Young socialist women are pushing the argument that conscription of women is important in the name of equality. At the same time, they also declare themselves antimilitarists, and say no to NATO. They also object to the current Norwegian participation in the war in Afghanistan. Their arguments are the same as *Alice Schwarzer*'s thirty years ago and *Alice Miller*'s today, though there are certain nuances, as *Alice Schwarzer* would declare herself a conscientious objector (in the narrow sense), while *Alice Miller* would not. The older generation of antimilitarists in Norway reject the possibility of changing the military from within. On the contrary, they think that the idea of women *"making it softer"* is a contradiction. To accept conscription for men and women alike means an acceptance of the military as an institution, and militarism in general. Having more women in the military will more likely increase militarism throughout society. However, there is an openness to conscription for men and women within the broader concept of defence, which would allow for alternative peace service and training for nonviolent defence [6].

In Norway, UN Resolution 1325 on Women, Peace and Security is used to legitimise the need to recruit women into active military service, and it is argued further that men and women complement each other. The argument for recruiting women is that they are best fitted to meet traumatised women in war zones. This argument was also used by the former Minister of Defence, *Anne-Grete Strøm-Erichsen* [7].

A Norwegian researcher on culture and language, *Berit von der Lippe* [8], analysed the debate by looking at the concepts used to legitimise women's participation in the military, especially abroad. She looks at words used like *"human security"*, *"moral obligations"*, *"contributing to peace and conflict resolutions"*. She writes that the Ministry of Defence is legitimising the introduction of conscription of women in the name of democracy and human rights. This picture disguises what is actually happening, she argues, as war and occupation are within the totally different sphere of power-politics led by men. She thinks that conscripting women to serve in the military equalises them as aggressors who maintain a post-colonial attitude that has no perspective of the situation of women outside the West.

We expect this debate to be taken up in many other countries. Although it is linked to the debate about conscription in Norway, the arguments will be the same regarding the importance of having women in a professional army. To us, it also means that women's objection to militarism will be as important as ever. We also see that the language used by the Western military disguises its real meaning by talking about the good intentions of humanitarian wars, peacekeeping armies, wars for democracy, and being against terrorism. It may be that the open aggressiveness and masculinity in the military is more visible in countries other than Norway. *Cynthia Cockburn* [9] writes that human wars are about violence, and violence breeds violence.

The Future of Women's Conscientious Objection

We find that the contributors make strong arguments as to why they declare themselves conscientious objectors. One reason why we find this kind of activism encouraging is their very clear antimilitarist stand. By adopting a term that most people define in a very narrow sense, twisting it, expanding it, and giving it a much broader definition, the women manage to explain the problem of militarism very clearly, and link it closely to patriarchy, hierarchy and violence. In our understanding, the contributors take the concept back to peace activism where it belongs. *Cynthia Enloe* in her preface points at how women are openly investigating patriarchy's daily operations within national and international conscientious objection movements. These movements have helped to persuade many men considering conscientious objection to seriously confront their own behaviour in particular forms of patriarchal masculinity.

Conscientious objection implies much more than refusal to do military service. It can include objection for reasons of conscience to war and war preparation as well. The fact that conscientious objection is today used as a legal concept by the military in some countries is owed not to the good will of the military but to the strong demands by conscientious objectors and their supporters for a means to be heard and defended. Declaring oneself a conscientious objector is at the same time a very personal stand, and a principled stand against militarism as a root cause of many of the world's problems.

Most of the examples of women declaring themselves conscientious objectors seem to happen in highly militarised societies. Does this reflect the fact that it is *"easier"* to take a stand against militarism when it is visible, than when its effects are more subtle? Or is it just a coincidence? We don't know, but we suspect this might be the case. We also hope that by publishing this book we have helped make these women visible, so that their actions can serve as an inspiration to women against militarism in societies where militarism is less visible. However, we don't suggest just copying statements in this book. We do suggest that women reflect on the best way to counter the militarism of the state in their own countries. In many places without conscription, it will probably make good sense to consider this in mixed movements. In places that have recently abolished conscription for men, like many European states, it might be possible to build on structures and experiences from earlier conscientious objection movements. Or it might be necessary to build new networks. For a feminist critic of militarism, it might even work better to take feminist organisations as a point of departure. However, since the militarisation of our societies is damaging to both men and women, it might be well to include men in the refusal as well. Issue Number One will be to identify how militarism, and its *"cousins"* patriarchy and sexism, affect each woman's personal relationships as well as her relationship to the larger society. Issue Number Two will be to find like-minded people to work with and agree the best strategy for countering militarism where they live. Perhaps the first action should be to highlight the connections between militarism, patriarchy and sexism.

Women who call themselves conscientious objectors will probably remain a minority within the peace and feminist movements for a long time. It remains to be seen if the minority will grow. It might be useful for women conscientious objectors to see whether it is possible to identify a common platform that all can agree to and work from, in spite of all the different faces of militarism they are facing. This way, we think that a handful of women here and there will feel less isolated, and together they can contribute to a common analysis of militarism which is not restricted to militarism in one state, but the militarisation of the world. WRI, with its history of radical resistance to militarism and support for conscientious objectors, has the possibility of playing an important part in developing this analysis and support network.

The contributions presented here describe women's experiences as conscientious objectors within each woman's context. The stories are from different parts of the world, written independently from each other, though they show the same sort of development and are very similar in concept. But we find it striking that none of them refers to each other. As *Cynthia Enloe* points out, when women act as a collective, they often unearth new curiosities, new investigations, new awareness and new consciousness. So we conclude with the hope that this anthology can inspire women to embrace a new collective conscience against militarism and war.

Footnotes

[1] Cynthia Cockburn: "From where we stand. War, Women's Activism & Feminist Analysis." Zed Books 2007.
[2] Helsinki Times 9 December 2009 and CO-update January 2010, No. 53
[3] Mathiesen, Thomas "Makt og motmakt", [Power and counter-power], Pax forlag, Oslo 1982
[4] Spare Rib, March 1981.
[5] Cynthia Enloe: "Does Khaki become you? The Militarisation of Women's Lives." London, Pluto Press 1983; Cockburn op.cit.; Helen Benedict, Army Cpt. Jennifer Machmer: "Why Soldiers Rape. Culture of misogyny, illegal occupation, fuel sexual violence in military." http://www.inthesetimes.com/article/3848/ Downloaded 14 August 2008.
[6] Letter from Norwegian Section of WILPF to the Norwegian Minister of Defence, Anne-Grete Strøm-Erichsen, 28 May 2009.
[7] She was the Minister of Defence in the period 2005-2009.
[8] Klassekampen, 10 April 2007,
[9] Cynthia Cockburn: "From where we stand. War, Women's Activism & Feminist Analysis." Zed Books 2007.

Other War Resisters' International Publications

Handbook for Nonviolent Campaigns

ISBN 978-0-903517-21-8
January 2009, 152 pages, £5

Social change doesn't just happen. It's the result of the work of committed people striving for a world of justice and peace. This work gestates in groups or cells of activists, in discussions, in training sessions, in reflecting on previous experiences, in planning, in experimenting, and in learning from others. Preparing ourselves for our work for social justice is key to its success.
This Handbook shares what people have already developed in different contexts.

War is a Crime Against Humanity

The Story of War Resisters' International

By Devi Prasad
ISBN 978-0-903517-20-1
2005, 558 pages, £18

This history traces the development of the WRI from a movement centrally concerned with individual conscientious objection to war to one which combines this concern with a commitment to promoting collective nonviolent action against both war and oppression.

Visit War Resisters' International at http://wri-irg.org for more information

About War Resisters' International

War Resisters' International was founded in 1921 under the name "Paco". It was and is based on the WRI declaration:

> War is a crime against humanity. I am therefore determined not to support any kind of war, and to strive for the removal of all causes of war.

War Resisters' International exists to promote nonviolent action against the causes of war, and to support and connect people around the world who refuse to take part in war or the preparation of war. On this basis, WRI works for a world without war.

Nonviolence

WRI embraces nonviolence. For some, nonviolence is a way of life. For all of us, it is a form of action that affirms life, speaks out against oppression, and acknowledges the value of each person.

Nonviolence can combine active resistance, including civil disobedience, with dialogue; it can combine noncooperation — withdrawal of support from a system of oppression — with constructive work to build alternatives.

As a way of engaging in conflict, nonviolence attempts to empower those at the bottom of society and include people from different sides in seeking a solution.

No to war

WRI will never endorse any kind of war, whether it is waged by a state, by a "*liberation army*", or under the auspices of the United Nations, even if it is called a "*humanitarian military intervention*". Wars, however noble the rhetoric, invariably are used to serve some power-political or economic interest. We know where war leads — to suffering and destruction, to rape and organised crime, to betrayal of values and to new structures of domination.

Contact:

War Resisters' International
5 Caledonian Road
London N1 9DX
Britain
Email info@wri-irg.org
Web http://wri-irg.org